Ha
Bus.....
Review

ON

BUILDING PERSONAL AND
ORGANIZATIONAL RESILIENCE

THE HARVARD BUSINESS REVIEW PAPERBACK SERIES

The series is designed to bring today's managers and professionals the fundamental information they need to stay competitive in a fast-moving world. From the preeminent thinkers whose work has defined an entire field to the rising stars who will redefine the way we think about business, here are the leading minds and landmark ideas that have established the *Harvard Business Review* as required reading for ambitious businesspeople in organizations around the globe.

Other books in the series:

Harvard Business Review Interviews with CEOs

Harvard Business Review on Advances in Strategy

Harvard Business Review on Becoming a High Performance Manager

Harvard Business Review on Brand Management

Harvard Business Review on Breakthrough Leadership

Harvard Business Review on Breakthrough Thinking

Harvard Business Review on Business and the Environment

Harvard Business Review on the Business Value of IT

Harvard Business Review on Change

Harvard Business Review on Compensation

Harvard Business Review on Corporate Ethics

Harvard Business Review on Corporate Governance

Harvard Business Review on Corporate Responsibility

Harvard Business Review on Corporate Strategy

Harvard Business Review on Crisis Management

Harvard Business Review on Culture and Change

Harvard Business Review on Customer Relationship Management

Harvard Business Review on Decision Making

Harvard Business Review on Effective Communication

Other books in the series (continued):

Harvard Business Review

ON

BUILDING PERSONAL AND ORGANIZATIONAL RESILIENCE

A HARVARD BUSINESS REVIEW PAPERBACK

The *Harvard Business Review* articles in this collection are available as individual reprints. Discounts apply to quantity purchases. For information and ordering, please contact Customer Service, Harvard Business School Publishing, Boston, MA 02163. Telephone: (617) 783-7500 or (800) 988-0886, 8 A.M. to 6 P.M. Eastern Time, Monday through Friday. Fax: (617) 783-7555, 24 hours a day. E-mail: custserv@hbsp.harvard.edu

Library of Congress Cataloging-in-Publication Data
Harvard business review on building personal and organizational resilience.
        p.   cm. — (The Harvard business review paperback series)
        Includes index.
        ISBN 1-59139-272-1 (alk. paper)
        1. Crisis management.   2. Leadership.   3. Resilience (Personality trait).   4. Organizational change.   5. Success in business—Psychological aspects.   I. Harvard business review.   II. Series.
HD49.H368   2003
658.4´056—dc21   2003008214
                                                                                    CIP

The paper used in this publication meets the requirements of the American National Standard for Permanence of Paper for Publications and Documents in Libraries and Archives Z39.48-1992.

Contents

Harvard Business Review

ON

BUILDING PERSONAL AND
ORGANIZATIONAL RESILIENCE

How Resilience Works

DIANE L. COUTU

Executive Summary

WHY DO SOME PEOPLE BOUNCE back from life's hardships while others despair? HBR senior editor Diane Coutu looks at the nature of individual and organizational resilience, issues that have gained special urgency in light of the recent terrorist attacks, war, and recession. In the business arena, resilience has found its way onto the list of qualities sought in employees. As one of Coutu's interviewees puts it, "More than education, more than experience, more than training, a person's level of resilience will determine who succeeds and who fails."

Theories abound about what produces resilience, but three fundamental characteristics seem to set resilient people and companies apart from others. One or two of these qualities make it possible to bounce back from hardship, but true resilience requires all three.

The first characteristic is the capacity to accept and face down reality. In looking hard at reality, we prepare ourselves to act in ways that allow us to endure and survive hardships: We train ourselves how to survive before we ever have to do so.

Second, resilient people and organizations possess an ability to find meaning in some aspects of life. And values are just as important as meaning; value systems at resilient companies change very little over the long haul and are used as scaffolding in times of trouble.

The third building block of resilience is the ability to improvise. Within an arena of personal capabilities or company rules, the ability to solve problems without the usual or obvious tools is a great strength.

W HEN I BEGAN MY CAREER in journalism—I was a reporter at a national magazine in those days—there was a man I'll call Claus Schmidt. He was in his mid-fifties, and to my impressionable eyes, he was the quintessential newsman: cynical at times, but unrelentingly curious and full of life, and often hilariously funny in a sandpaper-dry kind of way. He churned out hard-hitting cover stories and features with a speed and elegance I could only dream of. It always astounded me that he was never promoted to managing editor.

But people who knew Claus better than I did thought of him not just as a great newsman but as a quintessential survivor, someone who had endured in an environment often hostile to talent. He had lived through at least three major changes in the magazine's leadership, losing most of his best friends and colleagues on the way.

At home, two of his children succumbed to incurable illnesses, and a third was killed in a traffic accident. Despite all this—or maybe because of it—he milled around the newsroom day after day, mentoring the cub reporters, talking about the novels he was writing—always looking forward to what the future held for him.

Why do some people suffer real hardships and not falter? Claus Schmidt could have reacted very differently. We've all seen that happen: One person cannot seem to get the confidence back after a layoff; another, persistently depressed, takes a few years off from life after her divorce. The question we would all like answered is, Why? What exactly is that quality of resilience that carries people through life?

It's a question that has fascinated me ever since I first learned of the Holocaust survivors in elementary school. In college, and later in my studies as an affiliate scholar at the Boston Psychoanalytic Society and Institute, I returned to the subject. For the past several months, however, I have looked on it with a new urgency, for it seems to me that the terrorism, war, and recession of recent months have made understanding resilience more important than ever. I have considered both the nature of individual resilience and what makes some organizations as a whole more resilient than others. Why do some people and some companies buckle under pressure? And what makes others bend and ultimately bounce back?

My exploration has taught me much about resilience, although it's a subject none of us will ever understand fully. Indeed, resilience is one of the great puzzles of human nature, like creativity or the religious instinct. But in sifting through psychological research and in reflecting on the many stories of resilience I've heard, I have seen a little more deeply into the hearts and minds of people like Claus Schmidt and, in doing so, looked more deeply into the human psyche as well.

The Buzz About Resilience

Resilience is a hot topic in business these days. Not long ago, I was talking to a senior partner at a respected consulting firm about how to land the very best MBAs—the name of the game in that particular industry. The partner, Daniel Savageau (not his real name), ticked off a long list of qualities his firm sought in its hires: intelligence, ambition, integrity, analytic ability, and so on. "What about resilience?" I asked. "Well, that's very popular right now," he said. "It's the new buzzword. Candidates even tell us they're resilient; they volunteer the information. But frankly, they're just too young to know that about themselves. Resilience is something you realize you have *after* the fact."

"More than education, more than experience, more than training, a person's level of resilience will determine who succeeds and who fails. That's true in the cancer ward, it's true in the Olympics, and it's true in the boardroom."

"But if you could, would you test for it?" I asked. "Does it matter in business?"

Savageau paused. He's a man in his late forties and a success personally and professionally. Yet it hadn't been a smooth ride to the top. He'd started his life as a poor French Canadian in Woonsocket, Rhode Island, and had lost his father at six. He lucked into a football scholarship but was kicked out of Boston University twice for drinking. He turned his life around in his twenties, married, divorced, remarried, and raised five children. Along the way, he made and lost two fortunes before helping to found the consulting firm he now runs. "Yes, it does matter," he said at last. "In fact, it probably matters more than any of the usual things we look for." In the course of reporting this article, I heard the same assertion time and again. As Dean Becker, the president and CEO of Adaptiv Learning Systems, a four-year-old company in King of Prussia, Pennsylvania, that develops and delivers programs about resilience training, puts it: "More than education, more than experience, more than training, a person's level of resilience will determine who succeeds and who fails. That's true in the cancer ward, it's true in the Olympics, and it's true in the boardroom."

Academic research into resilience started about 40 years ago with pioneering studies by Norman Garmezy, now a professor emeritus at the University of Minnesota in Minneapolis. After studying why many children of schizophrenic parents did not suffer psychological illness as a result of growing up with them, he concluded that a certain quality of resilience played a greater role in mental health than anyone had previously suspected.

Today, theories abound about what makes resilience. Looking at Holocaust victims, Maurice Vanderpol, a former president of the Boston Psychoanalytic Society and Institute, found that many of the healthy survivors of concentration camps had what he calls a "plastic shield." The shield was comprised of several factors, including a sense of humor. Often the humor was black, but nonetheless it provided a critical sense of perspective. Other core characteristics that helped included the ability to form attachments to others and the possession of an inner psychological space that protected the survivors from the intrusions of abusive others. Research about other groups uncovered different qualities associated with resilience. The Search Institute, a Minneapolis-based nonprofit organization that focuses on resilience and youth, found that the more resilient kids have an uncanny ability to get adults to help them out. Still other research showed that resilient inner-city youth often have talents such as athletic abilities that attract others to them.

Many of the early theories about resilience stressed the role of genetics. Some people are just born resilient, so the arguments went. There's some truth to that, of course, but an increasing body of empirical evidence shows that resilience—whether in children, survivors of concentration camps, or businesses back from the brink—can be learned. For example, George Vaillant, the director of the Study of Adult Development at Harvard Medical School in Boston, observes that within various groups studied during a 60-year period, some people became markedly more resilient over their lifetimes. Other psychologists claim that unresilient people more easily develop resiliency skills than those with head starts.

Most of the resilience theories I encountered in my research make good common sense. But I also observed that almost all the theories overlap in three ways. Resilient people, they posit, possess three characteristics: a staunch acceptance of reality; a deep belief, often buttressed by strongly held values, that life is meaningful; and an uncanny ability to improvise. You can bounce back from hardship with just one or two of these qualities, but you will only be truly resilient with all three. These three characteristics hold true for resilient organizations as well. Let's take a look at each of them in turn.

Facing Down Reality

A common belief about resilience is that it stems from an optimistic nature. That's true but only as long as such optimism doesn't distort your sense of reality. In extremely adverse situations, rose-colored thinking can actually spell disaster. This point was made poignantly to me by management researcher and writer Jim Collins, who happened upon this concept while researching *Good to Great*, his book on how companies transform themselves out of mediocrity. Collins had a hunch (an exactly wrong hunch) that resilient companies were filled with optimistic people. He tried out that idea on Admiral Jim Stockdale, who was held prisoner and tortured by the Vietcong for eight years.

Collins recalls: "I asked Stockdale: 'Who didn't make it out of the camps?' And he said, 'Oh, that's easy. It was the optimists. They were the ones who said we were going to be out by Christmas. And then they said we'd be out by Easter and then out by Fourth of July and out by Thanksgiving, and then it was Christmas again.' Then Stockdale turned to me and said, 'You know, I think they all died of broken hearts.'"

In the business world, Collins found the same unblinking attitude shared by executives at all the most successful companies he studied. Like Stockdale, resilient people have very sober and down-to-earth views of those parts of reality that matter for survival. That's not to say that optimism doesn't have its place: In turning around a demoralized sales force, for instance, conjuring a sense of possibility can be a very powerful tool. But for bigger challenges, a cool, almost pessimistic, sense of reality is far more important.

Perhaps you're asking yourself, "Do I truly understand—and accept—the reality of my situation? Does my
organization?" Those are good questions, particularly
because research suggests most people slip into denial as
a coping mechanism. Facing reality, really facing it, is
grueling work. Indeed, it can be unpleasant and often
emotionally wrenching. Consider the following story of
organizational resilience, and see what it means to confront reality.

Prior to September 11, 2001, Morgan Stanley, the
famous investment bank, was the largest tenant in the
World Trade Center. The company had some 2,700
employees working in the south tower on 22 floors
between the 43rd and the 74th. On that horrible day, the
first plane hit the north tower at 8:46 am, and Morgan
Stanley started evacuating just one minute later, at 8:47
am. When the second plane crashed into the south tower
15 minutes after that, Morgan Stanley's offices were
largely empty. All told, the company lost only seven
employees despite receiving an almost direct hit.

Of course, the organization was just plain lucky to be
in the second tower. Cantor Fitzgerald, whose offices
were hit in the first attack, couldn't have done anything
to save its employees. Still, it was Morgan Stanley's hard-
nosed realism that enabled the company to benefit from
its luck. Soon after the 1993 attack on the World Trade
Center, senior management recognized that working in
such a symbolic center of U.S. commercial power made
the company vulnerable to attention from terrorists and
possible attack.

With this grim realization, Morgan Stanley launched
a program of preparedness at the micro level. Few companies take their fire drills seriously. Not so Morgan
Stanley, whose VP of security for the Individual Investor

Group, Rick Rescorla, brought a military discipline to the job. Rescorla, himself a highly resilient, decorated Vietnam vet, made sure that people were fully drilled about what to do in a catastrophe. When disaster struck on September 11, Rescorla was on a bullhorn telling Morgan Stanley employees to stay calm and follow their well-practiced drill, even though some building supervisors were telling occupants that all was well. Sadly, Rescorla himself, whose life story has been widely covered in recent months, was one of the seven who didn't make it out.

"When you're in financial services where so much depends on technology, contingency planning is a major part of your business," says President and COO Robert G. Scott. But Morgan Stanley was prepared for the very toughest reality. It had not just one, but three, recovery sites where employees could congregate and business could take place if work locales were ever disrupted. "Multiple backup sites seemed like an incredible extravagance on September 10," concedes Scott. "But on September 12, they seemed like genius."

Maybe it was genius; it was undoubtedly resilience at work. The fact is, when we truly stare down reality, we prepare ourselves to act in ways that allow us to endure and survive extraordinary hardship. We train ourselves how to survive before the fact.

The Search for Meaning

The ability to see reality is closely linked to the second building block of resilience, the propensity to make meaning of terrible times. We all know people who, under duress, throw up their hands and cry, "How can this be happening to me?" Such people see themselves as victims, and living through hardship carries no lessons for them. But resilient people devise constructs about their suffering to create some sort of meaning for themselves and others.

I have a friend I'll call Jackie Oiseaux who suffered repeated psychoses over a ten-year period due to an undiagnosed bipolar disorder. Today, she holds down a big job in one of the top publishing companies in the country, has a family, and is a prominent member of her church community. When people ask her how she bounced back from her crises, she runs her hands through her hair. "People sometimes say, 'Why me?' But I've always said, 'Why *not* me?' True, I lost many things during my illness," she says, "but I found many more— incredible friends who saw me through the bleakest times and who will give meaning to my life forever."

This dynamic of meaning making is, most researchers agree, the way resilient people build bridges from present-day hardships to a fuller, better constructed future. Those bridges make the present manageable, for lack of a better word, removing the sense that the present is overwhelming. This concept was beautifully articulated by Viktor E. Frankl, an Austrian psychiatrist and an Auschwitz survivor. In the midst of staggering suffering, Frankl invented "meaning therapy," a humanistic therapy technique that helps individuals make the kinds of decisions that will create significance in their lives.

In his book *Man's Search for Meaning*, Frankl described the pivotal moment in the camp when he developed meaning therapy. He was on his way to work one day, worrying whether he should trade his last cigarette for a bowl of soup. He wondered how he was going to work with a new foreman whom he knew to be particularly sadistic. Suddenly, he was disgusted by just how trivial and meaningless his life had become. He realized that to survive, he had to find some purpose. Frankl did so by imagining himself giving a lecture after the war on the psychology of the concentration camp, to help outsiders understand what he had been through. Although he wasn't even sure he would survive, Frankl created some concrete goals for himself. In doing so, he succeeded in rising above the sufferings of the moment. As he put it in his book: "We must never forget that we may also find meaning in life even when confronted with a hopeless situation, when facing a fate that cannot be changed."

Frankl's theory underlies most resilience coaching in business. Indeed, I was struck by how often businesspeople referred to his work. "Resilience training—what we call hardiness—is a way for us to help people construct meaning in their everyday lives," explains Salvatore R. Maddi, a University of California, Irvine psychology professor and the director of the Hardiness Institute in Newport Beach, California. "When people realize the power of resilience training, they often say, 'Doc, is this what psychotherapy is?' But psychotherapy is for people whose lives have fallen apart badly and need repair. We see our work as showing people life skills and attitudes. Maybe those things should be taught at home, maybe they should be taught in schools, but they're not. So we end up doing it in business."

Yet the challenge confronting resilience trainers is often more difficult than we might imagine. Meaning can be elusive, and just because you found it once doesn't mean you'll keep it or find it again. Consider Aleksandr Solzhenitsyn, who survived the war against the Nazis, imprisonment in the gulag, and cancer. Yet when he moved to a farm in peaceful, safe Vermont, he could not cope with the "infantile West." He was unable to discern any real meaning in what he felt to be the destructive and irresponsible freedom of the West. Upset by his critics, he withdrew into his farmhouse, behind a locked fence, seldom to be seen in public. In 1994, a bitter man, Solzhenitsyn moved back to Russia.

Since finding meaning in one's environment is such an important aspect of resilience, it should come as no surprise that the most successful organizations and people possess strong value systems. Strong values infuse an environment with meaning because they offer ways to interpret and shape events. While it's popular these days to ridicule values, it's surely no coincidence that the most resilient organization in the world has been the Catholic Church, which has survived wars, corruption, and schism for more than 2,000 years, thanks largely to its immutable set of values. Businesses that survive also have their creeds, which give them purposes beyond just making money. Strikingly, many companies describe their value systems in religious terms. Pharmaceutical giant Johnson & Johnson, for instance, calls its value system, set out in a document given to every new employee at orientation, the Credo. Parcel company UPS talks constantly about its Noble Purpose.

Value systems at resilient companies change very little over the years and are used as scaffolding in times of trouble. UPS Chairman and CEO Mike Eskew believes that the Noble Purpose helped the company to rally after the agonizing strike in 1997. Says Eskew: "It was a hugely difficult time, like a family feud. Everyone had close friends on both sides of the fence, and it was tough for us to pick sides. But what

Resilience is neither ethically good nor bad. It is merely the skill and the capacity to be robust under conditions of enormous stress and change.

saved us was our Noble Purpose. Whatever side people were on, they all shared a common set of values. Those values are core to us and never change; they frame most of our important decisions. Our strategy and our mission may change, but our values never do."

The religious connotations of words like "credo," "values," and "noble purpose," however, should not be confused with the actual content of the values. Companies can hold ethically questionable values and still be very resilient. Consider Phillip Morris, which has demonstrated impressive resilience in the face of increasing unpopularity. As Jim Collins points out, Phillip Morris has very strong values, although we might not agree with them—for instance, the value of "adult choice." But there's no doubt that Phillip Morris executives believe strongly in its values, and the strength of their beliefs sets the company apart from most of the other tobacco companies. In this context, it is worth noting that resilience is neither ethically good nor bad. It is merely the skill and the capacity to be robust under conditions of enormous stress and change. As Viktor Frankl wrote: "On the average, only those prisoners could keep alive who, after years of trekking from camp to camp, had lost all scruples in their fight for existence; they were prepared to use every means, honest and otherwise, even brutal. . . , in order to save themselves. We who have come back . . . we know: The best of us did not return."

Values, positive or negative, are actually more important for organizational resilience than having resilient people on the payroll. If resilient employees are all interpreting reality in different ways, their decisions and actions may well conflict, calling into doubt the survival of their organization. And as the weakness of an organization becomes apparent, highly resilient individuals are more likely to jettison the organization than to imperil their own survival.

Ritualized Ingenuity

The third building block of resilience is the ability to make do with whatever is at hand. Psychologists follow the lead of French anthropologist Claude Levi-Strauss in calling this skill bricolage.[1] Intriguingly, the roots of that word are closely tied to the concept of resilience, which literally means "bouncing back." Says Levi-Strauss: "In its old sense, the verb *bricoler* . . . was always used with reference to some extraneous movement: a ball rebounding, a dog straying, or a horse swerving from its direct course to avoid an obstacle."

Bricolage in the modern sense can be defined as a kind of inventiveness, an ability to improvise a solution to a problem without proper or obvious tools or materials. *Bricoleurs* are always tinkering—building radios from household effects or fixing their own cars. They make the most of what they have, putting objects to unfamiliar uses. In the concentration camps, for example, resilient inmates knew to pocket pieces of string or wire whenever they found them. The string or wire might later become useful—to fix a pair of shoes, perhaps, which in freezing conditions might make the difference between life and death.

When situations unravel, bricoleurs muddle through, imagining possibilities where others are confounded. I have two friends, whom I'll call Paul Shields and Mike Andrews, who were roommates throughout their college years. To no one's surprise, when they graduated, they set up a business together, selling educational materials to schools, businesses, and consulting firms. At first, the

company was a great success, making both founders
paper millionaires. But the recession of the early 1990s
hit the company hard, and many core clients fell away.
At the same time, Paul experienced a bitter divorce and a
depression that made it impossible for him to work.
Mike offered to buy Paul out but was instead slapped
with a lawsuit claiming that Mike was trying to steal the
business. At this point, a less resilient person might have
just walked away from the mess. Not Mike. As the case
wound through the courts, he kept the company going
any way he could—constantly morphing the business
until he found a model that worked: going into joint ven-
tures to sell English-language training materials to Russian and Chinese companies. Later, he branched off into
publishing newsletters for clients. At one point, he was
even writing video scripts for his competitors. Thanks to
all this bricolage, by the time the lawsuit was settled in
his favor, Mike had an entirely different, and much more
solid, business than the one he had started with.

Bricolage can be practiced on a higher level as well.
Richard Feynman, winner of the 1965 Nobel Prize in
physics, exemplified what I like to think of as intellectual
bricolage. Out of pure curiosity, Feynman made himself
an expert on cracking safes, not only looking at the
mechanics of safecracking but also cobbling together
psychological insights about people who used safes and
set the locks. He cracked many of the safes at Los
Alamos, for instance, because he guessed that theoretical
physicists would not set the locks with random code
numbers they might forget but would instead use a
sequence with mathematical significance. It turned out
that the three safes containing all the secrets to the
atomic bomb were set to the same mathematical constant, e, whose first six digits are 2.71828.

Resilient organizations are stuffed with bricoleurs, though not all of them, of course, are Richard Feynmans. Indeed, companies that survive regard improvisation as a core skill. Consider UPS, which empowers its drivers to do whatever it takes to deliver packages on time. Says CEO Eskew: "We tell our employees to get the job done. If that means they need to improvise, they improvise. Otherwise we just couldn't do what we do every day. Just think what can go wrong: a busted traffic light, a flat tire, a bridge washed out. If a snowstorm hits Louisville tonight, a group of people will sit together and discuss how to handle the problem. Nobody tells them to do that. They come together because it's our tradition to do so."

That tradition meant that the company was delivering parcels in southeast Florida just one day after Hurricane Andrew devastated the region in 1992, causing billions of dollars in damage. Many people were living in their cars because their homes had been destroyed, yet UPS drivers and managers sorted packages at a diversion site and made deliveries even to those who were stranded in their cars. It was largely UPS's improvisational skills that enabled it to keep functioning after the catastrophic hit. And the fact that the company continued on gave others a sense of purpose or meaning amid the chaos.

Improvisation of the sort practiced by UPS, however, is a far cry from unbridled creativity. Indeed, much like the military, UPS lives on rules and regulations. As Eskew says: "Drivers always put their keys in the same place. They close the doors the same way. They wear their uniforms the same way. We are a company of precision." He believes that although they may seem stifling, UPS's rules were what allowed the company to bounce back immediately after Hurricane Andrew, for they enabled people to focus on the one or two fixes they needed to make in order to keep going.

Eskew's opinion is echoed by Karl E. Weick, a professor of organizational behavior at the University of Michigan Business School in Ann Arbor and one of the most respected thinkers on organizational psychology. "There is good evidence that when people are put under pressure, they regress to their most habituated ways of responding," Weick has written. "What we do not expect under life-threatening pressure is creativity." In other words, the rules and regulations that make some companies appear less creative may actually make them more resilient in times of real turbulence.

CLAUS SCHMIDT, THE NEWSMAN I mentioned earlier, died about five years ago, but I'm not sure I could have interviewed him about his own resilience even if he were alive. It would have felt strange, I think, to ask him, "Claus, did you really face down reality? Did you make meaning out of your hardships? Did you improvise your recovery after each professional and personal disaster?" He may not have been able to answer. In my experience, resilient people don't often describe themselves that way. They shrug off their survival stories and very often assign them to luck.

Obviously, luck does have a lot to do with surviving. It was luck that Morgan Stanley was situated in the south tower and could put its preparedness training to work. But being lucky is not the same as being resilient. Resilience is a reflex, a way of facing and understanding the world, that is deeply etched into a person's mind and soul. Resilient people and companies face reality with staunchness, make meaning of hardship instead of crying out in despair, and improvise solutions from thin air. Others do not. This is the nature of resilience, and we will never completely understand it.

Notes

1. See, e.g., Karl E. Weick, "The Collapse of Sensemaking in Organizations: The Mann Gulch Disaster," *Administrative Science Quarterly*, December 1993.

Originally published in May 2002
Reprint R0205B

Leading in Times of Trauma

JANE E. DUTTON, PETER J. FROST,
MONICA C. WORLINE, JACOBA M. LILIUS,
AND JASON M. KANOV

Executive Summary

AN EMPLOYEE IS DIAGNOSED with cancer or loses a family member unexpectedly. An earthquake destroys an entire section of a city, leaving hundreds dead, injured, or homeless. At times like these, managerial handbooks fail us. After all, leaders can't eliminate personal suffering, nor can they ask employees who are dealing with these crises to check their emotions at the door. But compassionate leadership can facilitate personal as well as organizational healing.

Based on research the authors have conducted at the University of Michigan and the University of British Columbia's CompassionLab, this article describes what leaders can do to foster organizational compassion in times of trauma. They recount real-world examples, including a story of personal tragedy at *Newsweek*, natural disasters that affected Macy's and Malden Mills, and the events of September 11, 2001.

During times of collective pain and confusion, compassionate leaders take some form of public action, however small, that is intended to ease people's pain and inspire others to act. By openly demonstrating their own humanity, executives can unleash a compassionate response throughout the whole company, increasing bonds among employees and attachments to the organization.

The authors say compassionate leaders uniformly provide two things: a "context for meaning"—creating an environment in which people can freely express and discuss how they feel—and a "context for action"—creating an environment in which those who experience or witness pain can find ways to alleviate their own and others' suffering.

A leader's competence in demonstrating and fostering compassion is vital, the authors conclude, to nourishing the very humanity that can make people—and organizations—great.

ONCE IN A GREAT WHILE, tragic circumstances present us with a challenge for which we simply cannot prepare. The terrorist attacks of last September immediately come to mind, but managers and their employees face crises at other times, too. Tragedies can occur at an individual level—an employee is diagnosed with cancer, for example, or loses a family member to an unexpected illness—or on a larger scale—a natural disaster destroys an entire section of a city, leaving hundreds of people dead, injured, or homeless. Such events can cause unspeakable pain not only for the people directly involved but also for those who see misfortune befall colleagues, friends, or even total strangers. That pain spills into the workplace. The managerial rule books fail us at times like these, when people are searching for meaning and a reason to hope for the future. There is, however, something leaders can do in times of collective pain and confusion. By the very nature of your position, you can help individuals and companies begin to heal by taking actions that demonstrate your own compassion, thereby unleashing a compassionate response throughout the whole organization. Our research at the University of Michigan and the University of British Columbia's CompassionLab has demonstrated that although the human capacity to show compassion is universal, some organizations suppress it while others create an environment in which compassion is not only expressed but spreads. (For more on our research, see "A Brief History of the CompassionLab" at the end of this article.)

Why is organizational compassion important, beyond the obvious and compelling reasons of humanity? Unleashing compassion in the workplace not only lessens the immediate suffering of those directly affected by trauma, it enables them to recover from future setbacks more quickly and effectively, and it increases their attachment to their colleagues and hence to the company itself. For those who witness or participate in acts of compassion, the effect is just as great; people's caring gestures contribute to their own resilience and attachment to the organization. Indeed, we've found that a leader's ability to enable a compassionate response throughout a company directly affects the organization's ability to maintain high performance in difficult times. It fosters a company's capacity to heal, to learn, to adapt, and to excel.

In the following pages, we will describe the actions leaders can take to enable organizational compassion in times of trauma. Before we begin, it's worth noting that some of our examples draw from the events of September 11, 2001, because the magnitude of pain surrounding those events was unprecedented in business history and because the public nature of those events makes the stories relevant to a broad audience. However, pain occurred in the workplace long before last September, and individual and group traumas will continue to disrupt people's daily routines—at times, shattering their lives—as long as humans continue to conduct business.

Beyond Empathy

When people think of compassion, the first thing that comes to mind for many is empathy. But while empathy can be comforting, it does not engender a broader response and therefore has limited capacity for organizational healing. Instead, our research shows that compassionate leadership involves taking some form of public action, however small, that is intended to ease people's pain—and that inspires others to act as well.

TJX president and CEO Edmond English, who lost seven employees aboard one of the planes that hit the World Trade Center, gathered his staff together shortly after the attacks to confirm the names of the victims. He called in grief counselors the very same day and chartered a plane to bring the victims' relatives from Canada and Europe to the company's headquarters in Framingham, Massachusetts. He personally greeted the families when they arrived in the parking lot at midnight on September 15. Although told by English that they could take some time off after the attacks, most employees opted to come in to work, as English himself had done, and support one another in the early days following the tragedy.

For a historical perspective on the same kind of compassionate leadership, we can look to Britain's Queen Mother, who demonstrated great courage by refusing to leave London as bombs ravaged the city around her during World War II. She and King George visited sites that had been destroyed during the Blitz of 1940, showing her dedication, concern, and commitment to the Allied cause, and inspiring lifelong admiration and loyalty for her constant presence.

In vivid contrast, immediately following the terrorist attacks in New York City, leaders at a publishing company close to ground zero refused to disrupt business as usual. The company held regularly scheduled meetings the day after the attacks and provided little or no support for people to share and express their pain. One editor told us she'd gotten a call at home early on the morning of September 12, just as she was trying to help her eight-year-old daughter make sense of what had happened the day before, demanding to know why she was late for a meeting. She went to work and sat through a four-hour conference call but was present in body only. Because she was given no opportunity to connect with her family, friends, and colleagues and was offered little organizational comfort in the face of a terrifying and confusing sequence of events, she felt her loyalty to the company eroding with every passing minute.

What English and other leaders have done—and what the leaders of the publishing company failed to do—is facilitate a compassionate institutional response on two levels. The first level is what we call a *context for meaning*—the leader creates an environment in which people can freely express and discuss the way they feel, which in turn helps them to make sense of their pain, seek or provide comfort, and imagine a more hopeful future. The second level is a *context for action*—the leader creates an environment in which those who experience or witness pain can find ways to alleviate their own and others' suffering. We have undertaken in-depth studies of leaders at organizations facing all manner of crises, and we have found that those who excel at leading compassionately and effectively in times of crisis adhere to a set of shared practices that help people make sense of terrible events and allow employees to move on.

Meaning amid Chaos

Acute trauma, tragedy, or distress can cause people to engage in intense soul-searching. We aren't referring to the restlessness and stock-taking that are a natural and ongoing process as people mature and grow in their careers; we're talking about the persistent and vexing questions that affect how people live their lives: Why did this happen? Could I have prevented it? How will we cope? Why me? And even, for employees who witness a tragic event but are not directly affected, why *not* me?

It isn't your job as a leader to answer these questions. But at the same time, it's not realistic or reasonable to ask people to ponder these questions only on their own time, outside the office. Instead, you can cultivate an environment that allows people to work through these questions in their own way so they can eventually start assigning meaning to events and begin healing.

You can start by setting an example for others by openly revealing your own humanity. You may well experience the same emotions affecting your employees—

from deep sorrow to anxiousness to uncertainty to anger to steely resolve. Openly expressing these feelings can be very powerful for those who witness it, especially during times of extreme pain. Mayor Rudolph Giuliani's public display of grief in the wake of the New York terrorist attacks set the stage for an honest expression of anguish throughout the city and, at the same time, strengthened people's resolve to rebuild and restore confidence in the city. When people know they can bring their pain to the office, they no longer have to expend energy trying to ignore or suppress it, and they can more easily and effectively get back to work. This may be a mutually reinforcing cycle, since getting back to a routine can be healing in itself.

When people know they can bring their pain to the office, they no longer have to expend energy trying to ignore or suppress it, and they can more easily and effectively get back to work.

Conversely, when you expect people to stifle their emotions, they don't know how and where to direct their energies, and it's very difficult for them to figure out how to focus at work. It can also test their loyalty to the organization. We interviewed employees at an architectural firm where a visitor died suddenly in the firm's hallways despite employees' heroic efforts to revive him. Company leaders did not acknowledge the trauma publicly, leaving people shocked and demoralized—and uncertain about how to respond should such an event occur again. Some employees were wracked with guilt over not being able to save the man's life. Others felt weak and helpless because they had no opportunity to grieve in the presence of their colleagues. They had shared a significant experience and could not console one another—or even recognize people's extraordinary efforts to revive the victim. This one event damaged not just the employees who were directly involved but also the social fabric of the whole company. By acting as if nothing out of the ordinary had happened, the company's leaders left people feeling as if the organization didn't recognize them as human beings, which created a rift between employees and management that has never been repaired.

A seemingly simple but important aspect of demonstrating your humanity is just being present, physically and emotionally. It shows employees that the organization cares about what happens to them and will do whatever it can to help them in a time of need. At one leading market-research firm, a senior executive died suddenly of a heart attack. The grief-stricken CEO personally visited each member of his 20-person management team to deliver the news, going house to house to share in each person's sorrow. His presence couldn't undo their colleague's death, nor could it stop their pain. But there is tremendous power in just sitting with people as they process terrible events. Bear in mind, too, that being there doesn't mean you have to visit people at home. Sitting with someone who's going through a crisis in his or her office can be just as powerful.

It isn't necessarily words that matter at times like these. Indeed, the dean of a divinity school told us that when a close relative died unexpectedly, he had been most comforted by one couple who arrived at his house and simply wept with him. To this day he remembers their very presence as a powerful moment of healing. Unfortunately, however, the simple act of being there doesn't come easily or naturally to most people. It can be much easier to avoid those who are in pain. One CEO in our research told us that his natural tendency had been to shrink from addressing people's personal problems—until the sudden death of his own son revealed for him the power of other people's presence.

Leaders can also help people in times of trauma by taking care of their basic needs, which gives people room to make meaning of events for themselves and allows them to focus on coping with the crisis. This is one reason people bring food to friends who have suffered a death in the family, but it can apply to organizations as well. At one consulting firm we studied, an employee's daughter suffered an horrific car accident far from home. To make it easier for the employee and her husband, the company's leaders rented an apartment for them near the hospital. Knowing that they had a safe and close place to stay removed one aspect of the family's stress and allowed them to focus on their daughter's health.

In another example, the wife of a terminally ill employee at Cisco Systems was so taxed with caring for her husband that she couldn't find the time to make him a pot roast, his favorite dinner, on his birthday. Barbara Beck, a senior vice president at the company, decided she would cook a pot roast and deliver it to the family herself. The gesture lent a semblance of normalcy to the occasion and gave the employee's wife the space she needed to cope with her husband's illness and to process its effects on her life. In yet another case, the branch manager at a bank, whose close friend and second-in-command died of a heart attack, took on numerous extra duties and clients so his employees would have additional time to mourn—even as he himself was suffering tremendous grief.

This meaning-making process can also be supported by communicating and reinforcing organizational values—reminding people about the larger purpose of their work even as they struggle to make sense of major life issues. When *Newsweek* employees were coping with the unexpected illness and death of editor Maynard Parker, the magazine's editor-in-chief, Richard Smith, at once emphasized the company's commitment to community and its commitment to remaining a world-class news-magazine. He created an environment in which people could do their best work and at the same time share their sorrow over Parker's losing battle with leukemia. Smith gave daily updates on Parker's condition and stressed that the company was actively involved in getting him top medical care. Knowing that they had ample opportunities to talk about their feelings, and that Parker was getting the best care possible, the *Newsweek* staff could then concentrate on honoring the publication's commitment to remaining a leading newsmagazine—which was particularly meaningful because Parker had so enthusiastically pursued this goal himself. The year's most significant news event was breaking just as Parker fell ill, and *Newsweek* emerged as a leader in the coverage in part because employees wanted to honor Parker in the way he would have valued most—by showing tremendous loyalty in an industry marked by high turnover.

Mark Whitaker, who was then managing editor and succeeded Parker as editor, has reflected on how Smith and others at the top of the organization provided meaning for people that could sustain them through the crisis and beyond. "I think it made people realize, 'Well, if I ever have a situation like that myself, God forbid, this is a company that will be there for me.' That is an intangible thing, but I think it's very powerful," Whitaker recalls. "The way that you deal with tragedy and illness and misfortune in the lives not only of your top people but of all your people really defines your values as an organization."

The Benjamin Group, a Silicon Valley–based public relations firm, demonstrates its values by taking a stand on how employees are treated not only by their colleagues and managers but also by their customers, suppliers, and other business partners. CEO Sheri Benjamin has established a code of principles that includes the statement "We're all in this together," and one implication is that if a client is consistently abusive to firm members, the firm will resign the account. A few years ago, the company dropped a million-dollar account—at that time, worth fully 20% of its annual business. Employees were startled that the firm would go so far, but they were energized, too: Inspired by the knowledge that the PR firm cared about their well-being, they worked extra hard to bring in new clients.

A final note on meaning-making: Symbolic gestures can be very powerful. Two days after the September 11 terrorist attacks, England's Queen Elizabeth II asked her troops to play *The Star-Spangled Banner* during the changing of the guard services outside Buckingham Palace. This extraordinary break from a time-honored tradition, dating back to 1660, gave thousands of Americans far from home, as well as supporters from other countries, a way to pay their respects and to mourn.

Actions amid Agony

A context for meaning is the all-important backdrop for creating a compassionate organization, but it is in creating a context for action that leaders can truly unleash an organization's power to heal. As a leader you can set the right example to awaken the potential for compassion, and you can prompt the organizational infrastructure to reinforce and institutionalize compassionate acts.

Perhaps the most important step you can take is to model the behaviors you would like to see others demonstrate. Frequently, people aren't sure if it's appropriate to bring personal matters into the workplace, or they may simply not know how. You can show them, using your status and visibility as a leader.

When a fire destroyed some student living quarters at the University of Michigan Business School, former dean B. Joseph White interrupted his annual "state of the

We've seen leaders redirect funds intended for other purposes to pay for grief counselors.

school" speech—typically heavily scripted and highly formal—with some strikingly personal remarks. He assured displaced students that the school would house them and wrote a personal check on the spot to pledge his support. Word of White's actions spread fast, catalyzing a campus-wide effort to tap alumni, faculty, and staff networks to find housing, financial support, and other resources for the students affected by the fire.

Leaders can also use their influence to reallocate resources to support people in need. We spoke with the manager of a billing department at one hospital who makes it a point to know the workloads and the personal circumstances of each member of her unit; that way, she can cut people slack when they need extra support. For example, when one employee's husband suffered kidney failure and was awaiting a transplant, the billing manager gave the woman a pager and organized a team of people who could step in and pick up the woman's work on a moment's notice. That way, the employee would be able to take her husband to the hospital without delay if a kidney became available.

In the wake of the September 11 attacks, the MWW Group, a public relations firm based in East Rutherford,

New Jersey, juggled its resources so that people could take time off to volunteer at relief organizations. We've also seen leaders redirect funds intended for other purposes to pay for grief counselors in times of collective trauma. When tragedy strikes, a company's existing infrastructure (its formal and informal networks and routines) can be helpful in locating useful resources, generating ideas, coordinating groups that are not typically connected, and communicating to people what is happening and how the company is responding. For example, after two Macy's stores were badly damaged in the 1994 Northridge, California, earthquake and could not immediately reopen, a store manager used the payroll system to quickly deliver cash to employees whose homes were destroyed. Macy's issued emergency advances of up to $1,000 at a time so that people could secure food, water, and shelter for their families. Following the immediate relief effort, the human resources team used its standard placement routines to search among Macy's stores in Southern California for opportunities to put displaced workers back on the job right away. HR workers quickly determined where help was most needed and then used their networks of employees to establish car pools for people. Within a short time, all employees and undamaged stores were up and running again. People often think of routines as unwieldy processes that interfere with quick response. But in Macy's case, as at other companies we've studied, the established routines helped to expedite matters.

Companies can also set up new routines or networks designed specifically to accelerate aid in the event of a crisis. After a Cisco employee developed a medical emergency while visiting Japan and couldn't find an English-speaking health care provider, the company wanted to make sure that no other employee would ever feel so alone in such a frightening circumstance. So it designed a network that would furnish medical assistance to any member of the Cisco family traveling abroad. Interestingly, that network has proved valuable in unexpected ways. In 1998, for instance, civil strife in Indonesia put Jakarta-based employees in the midst of conflict. The company Cisco used to provide international health services sent an ambulance to Cisco's Jakarta headquarters—an ambulance could travel through the streets where no ordinary car could. Employees were loaded into the ambulance, hidden beneath blankets, and driven to a deserted army airstrip where a waiting aircraft took them to safety.

From the Bottom Up

It's essential to note that organizational response doesn't have to start at the top. Leaders need to recognize and support instances where spontaneous organizing and compassionate actions occur at the lower levels of a company. When the organizational context emphasizes and inspires compassionate responses, bottom-up initiatives can take hold and have a transformative effect. Indeed, much of the assistance following the fire at the University of Michigan was generated by staff and students. One student, who did not even know the victims very well, organized more than 40 other students to recreate all the classroom notes from two years of MBA studies and delivered the study materials to the victims within a week of the fire.

At Foote Hospital in Jackson, Michigan, employees wanted to help a colleague who had lost three close relatives, so they lobbied for a system that would let them donate vacation or personal time to others who needed extra days off. Donating time has now become an official policy at Foote—although, of course, contributions are voluntary—thanks to the initiative and innovative thinking of people at the staff level of the organization. This program took on new life in the wake of the attacks in New York and Washington, DC. Foote employees donated more than $18,000 worth of their vacation time to the Red Cross relief fund—again, at their own initiative—and the hospital matched this amount.

At *Newsweek*, one employee organized a blood and platelet donation drive when Maynard Parker fell ill, another managed home chores for Parker's family, and yet another babysat his children. Another bottom-up response arose when Morgan Stanley was devastated by the World Trade Center attacks and had no immediate way to keep track of who was affected. Customer-service representatives from another division of the company took the initiative to organize a vital service: They collected employee information and created a Web site to help the company respond to the needs of individual families.

As these stories show, organizational compassion can be contagious. Indeed, what we call "positive spirals of compassion," where one act of compassion inspires another, are common. At the University of Michigan, for example, MBA students organized a fund-raiser to support victims of the huge earthquake in India last May. When they heard about the relief effort, the leaders of several student clubs contributed the remainder of their club budgets to the drive. (See "Measuring Organizational Compassion" at the end of this article for more information.)

The Case for Compassion

It's hard to document the positive effect that organizational compassion has on employee retention and productivity, but it's clear that employees will reward companies that treat them humanely. On December 11, 1995, a fire destroyed the Malden Mills manufacturing plant in Massachusetts. Instead of taking his $300 million insurance payout and relocating or retiring, owner Aaron Feuerstein decided to rebuild the factory. He announced that he would keep all 3,000 employees on the payroll through December while he started to rebuild. In January, he said he would pay them for a second month, and in February, Feuerstein pledged to pay for a third. His generosity made quite an impact on his employees: Productivity at the plant nearly doubled once it reopened.

Conversely, the costs of not providing leadership and the organizational infrastructure to help people deal with their grief are considerable. People in pain tend to be distracted at work, and if they don't have appropriate outlets, they may become unresponsive and even uncooperative in dealing with colleagues and customers. Just as compassion can be contagious, so can the detachment that accompanies a noncompassionate response; loyalty to the organization erodes not just among people who have directly suffered a tragedy but also among their colleagues who witness the lack of care. Over time, if an organization will not or cannot support the healing process, employee retention will suffer.

At one newspaper, a newsroom manager lost his wife to breast cancer. During his wife's extended illness, the employee felt no compassion from his boss; instead he endured complaints about his relatively low level of production. On his first day back to work after the funeral his boss said, "I guess you'll be working those 12-hour days again." The journalist, who was now raising two young children on his own, quit.

In another example, a health care employee finally got pregnant after many years of trying, only to deliver a stillborn baby in her eighth month. When the woman's boss stopped by her hospital room, she assumed he was there to offer his condolences. Instead he had come to ask her when she would return to work. Shocked at his lack of compassion, the woman applied to be transferred to another unit, and her manager—who ran a very busy and stretched unit—lost a valued employee with more than ten years of experience.

As a colleague of ours once remarked, there is always grief somewhere in the room. One person may be feeling personal pain due to a death in the family. Another may find personality conflicts in the workplace unbearable. Still another may be watching a colleague struggle with a serious illness and not know how to help. You can't eliminate such suffering, nor can you ask people to check their emotions at the door. But you can use your leadership to begin the healing process. Through your presence you can model behaviors that set the stage for the process of making meaning out of terrible events. And through your actions you can empower people to find their own ways to support one another during painful times. This is a kind of leadership we wish we would never have to use, yet it is vital if we are to nourish the very humanity that can make people—and organizations—great.

A Brief History of the CompassionLab

THIS ARTICLE IS BASED ON three years of research conducted at the CompassionLab, a joint project of the University of Michigan Business School and the

University of British Columbia. We began our work in 1998, based on a common interest in the way that stories of compassionate acts could inspire further acts of compassion. Over the next couple of years, we began to explore how different organizations deal with pain and compassion, and we found stunning differences in their capacity for compassion. This capacity turned out to have a direct impact on how quickly and effectively people in those organizations were able to recover from tragic events.

To learn more, we conducted extended studies on the life spans of painful events—for instance, serious illness, death, and violent acts—tracing the organizational response from the onset of the events. We interviewed the people directly affected, as well as those who witnessed others' suffering, to learn how organizations can encourage or suppress the healing process. Recently, we've been looking at how the degree of organizational compassion in a company affects employee retention. We're also conducting in-depth studies in which we observe everyday acts of compassion in an effort to understand which actions enable and which hinder healing.

Our research took on added urgency after September 11, 2001. As the effects of this trauma and pain continue to unfold, we wanted to share our findings to date.

Measuring Organizational Compassion

FOR A QUICK, HIGH-LEVEL CHECK on your organization's capacity for compassion, consider how it performs on the following four dimensions. Each indicator is a measure of the organization's compassion competence, which helps people to heal and continue on with their work when times are bad:

The *scope* of compassionate response refers to the breadth of resources provided to people in need, such as money, work flexibility, physical aid, and other people's time and attention. If an employee falls ill, is time off the only support, or does the system supply a wide range of healing resources such as variable work hours, gestures of comfort (like food, flowers, and cards), financial support, and assistance with child care?

The *scale* of compassionate response gauges the volume of resources, time, and attention that people who are suffering receive. Companies that are most effective at unleashing organizational compassion match the scale to the need. When a block of apartments was destroyed in a fire, the people who lived in the apartments, who worked for different companies, found a wide variation in how their companies responded. Some received a routine distribution of insurance coverage. Others were astonished at the outpouring of help from both corporate channels and individual colleagues—money, housewares, furniture, and offers of places to stay. In the latter case, the compassion competence of the system is more likely to help employees heal faster even as it strengthens their loyalty to the company—among those who experienced the tragedy directly and among those who witnessed and participated in the response.

Speed of response can vary widely as well. Companies with a competence for compassion extract and direct resources quickly, with little hesitation. Responding compassionately is a hardwired capability. Even in highly regimented bureaucracies, compassion can kick in quickly. In one manufacturing organization, a manager suffered a severe head injury that required almost three months of recovery. This was just after he had been appointed to lead an important experimental project that removed him from the regular compensation scheme and placed him on an incentive pay and benefits system. His previous job had been filled, and he was effectively stuck in no-man's land. A senior operations manager swiftly reinstated the man's previous compensation, obtaining the necessary sign-off without delay, an act that allayed the family's anxiety over its financial circumstances.

Specialization measures the degree to which the system customizes resources to the particular needs of an individual or a group in pain. If, for example, several employees' children are injured in a bus accident, some families will need close communication and hands-on comforting. Others will need to grieve privately and get back to work quickly.

Originally published in January 2002
Reprint R0201D

Crucibles of Leadership

WARREN G. BENNIS AND
ROBERT J. THOMAS

Executive Summary

WHAT MAKES A GREAT LEADER? Why do some people appear to know instinctively how to inspire employees—bringing out their confidence, loyalty, and dedication—while others flounder again and again?

No simple formula can explain how great leaders come to be, but Bennis and Thomas believe it has something to do with the ways people handle adversity. The authors' recent research suggests that one of the most reliable indicators and predictors of true leadership is the ability to learn from even the most negative experiences. An extraordinary leader is a kind of phoenix rising from the ashes of adversity stronger and more committed than ever.

In interviewing more than 40 leaders in business and the public sector over the past three years, the authors discovered that all of them—young and old alike—had endured intense, often traumatic, experiences that transformed them and became the source of their distinctive leadership abilities.

Bennis and Thomas call these shaping experiences "crucibles," after the vessels medieval alchemists used in their attempts to turn base metals into gold. For the interviewees, their crucibles were the points at which they were forced to question who they were and what was important to them. These experiences made them stronger and more confident and changed their sense of purpose in some fundamental way.

Through a variety of examples, the authors explore the idea of the crucible in detail. They also reveal that great leaders possess four essential skills, the most critical of which is "adaptive capacity"—an almost magical ability to transcend adversity and emerge stronger than before.

As LIFELONG STUDENTS of leadership, we are fascinated with the notion of what makes a leader. Why is it that certain people seem to naturally inspire confidence, loyalty, and hard work, while others (who may have just as much vision and smarts) stumble, again and again? It's a timeless question, and there's no simple answer. But we have come to believe it has something to do with the different ways that people deal with adversity. Indeed, our recent research has led us to conclude that one of the most reliable indicators and predictors of true leadership is an individual's ability to find meaning in negative events and to learn from even the most trying circumstances. Put another way, the skills required to conquer adversity and emerge stronger and more committed than ever are the same ones that make for extraordinary leaders.

Take Sidney Harman. Thirty-four years ago, the then-48-year-old businessman was holding down two executive positions. He was the chief executive of Harman Kardon (now Harman International), the audio components company he had cofounded, and he was serving as president of Friends World College, now Friends World Program, an experimental Quaker school on Long Island whose essential philosophy is that students, not their teachers, are responsible for their education. Juggling the two jobs, Harman was living what he calls a "bifurcated life," changing clothes in his car and eating lunch as he drove between Harman Kardon offices and plants and the Friends World campus. One day while at the college, he was told his company's factory in Bolivar, Tennessee, was having a crisis.

He immediately rushed to the Bolivar factory, a facility that was, as Harman now recalls, "raw, ugly, and, in many ways, demeaning." The problem, he found, had erupted in the polish and buff department, where a crew of a dozen workers, mostly African-Americans, did the dull, hard work of polishing mirrors and other parts, often under unhealthy conditions. The men on the night shift were supposed to get a coffee break at 10 pm. When the buzzer that announced the workers' break went on the fritz, management arbitrarily decided to postpone the break for ten minutes, when another buzzer was scheduled to sound. But one worker, "an old black man with an almost biblical name, Noah B. Cross," had "an epiphany," as Harman describes it. "He said, literally, to his fellow workers, 'I don't work for no buzzer. The buzzer works for me. It's my job to tell me when it's ten o'clock. I got me a watch. I'm not waiting another ten minutes. I'm going on my coffee break.' And all 12 guys took their coffee break, and, of course, all hell broke loose."

The worker's principled rebellion—his refusal to be cowed by management's senseless rule—was, in turn, a revelation to Harman: "The technology is there to serve the men, not the reverse," he remembers realizing. "I suddenly had this awakening that everything I was doing at the college had appropriate applications in business." In the ensuing years, Harman revamped the factory and its workings, turning it into a kind of campus—offering classes on the premises, including piano lessons, and encouraging the workers to take most of the responsibility for running their workplace. Further, he created an environment where dissent was not only tolerated but also encouraged. The plant's lively independent newspaper, the *Bolivar Mirror*, gave workers a creative and emotional outlet—and they enthusiastically skewered Harman in its pages.

Harman had, unexpectedly, become a pioneer of participative management, a movement that continues to influence the shape of workplaces around the world. The concept wasn't a grand idea conceived in the CEO's office and imposed on the plant, Harman says. It grew organically out of his going down to Bolivar to, in his words, "put out this fire." Harman's

The skills required to conquer adversity and emerge stronger and more committed than ever are the same ones that make for extraordinary leaders.

transformation was, above all, a creative one. He had connected two seemingly unrelated ideas and created a radically different approach to management that recognized both the economic and humane benefits of a more collegial workplace. Harman went on to accomplish far more during his career. In addition to founding Harman International, he served as the deputy secretary of commerce under Jimmy Carter. But he always looked back on the incident in Bolivar as the formative event in his professional life, the moment he came into his own as a leader.

The details of Harman's story are unique, but their significance is not. In interviewing more than 40 top leaders in business and the public sector over the past three years, we were surprised to find that all of them—young and old—were able to point to intense, often traumatic, always unplanned experiences that had transformed them and had become the sources of their distinctive leadership abilities.

We came to call the experiences that shape leaders "crucibles," after the vessels medieval alchemists used in their attempts to turn base metals into gold. For the leaders we interviewed, the crucible experience was a trial and a test, a point of deep self-reflection that forced them to question who they were and what mattered to them. It required them to examine their values, question their assumptions, hone their judgment. And, invariably, they emerged from the crucible stronger and more sure of themselves and their purpose—changed in some fundamental way.

Leadership crucibles can take many forms. Some are violent, life-threatening events. Others are more prosaic episodes of self-doubt. But whatever the crucible's nature, the people we spoke with were able, like Harman, to create a narrative around it, a story of how they were challenged, met the challenge, and became better leaders. As we studied these stories, we found that they not only told us how individual leaders are shaped but also pointed to some characteristics that seem common to all leaders—characteristics that were formed, or at least exposed, in the crucible.

Learning from Difference

A crucible is, by definition, a transformative experience through which an individual comes to a new or an altered sense of identity. It is perhaps not surprising then that one of the most common types of crucibles we documented involves the experience of prejudice. Being a victim of prejudice is particularly traumatic because it forces an individual to confront a distorted picture of him- or herself, and it often unleashes profound feelings of anger, bewilderment, and even withdrawal. For all its trauma, however, the experience of prejudice is for some a clarifying event. Through it, they gain a clearer vision of who they are, the role they play, and their place in the world.

Consider, for example, Liz Altman, now a Motorola vice president, who was transformed by the year she spent at a Sony camcorder factory in rural Japan, where she faced both estrangement and sexism. It was, says Altman, "by far, the hardest thing I've ever done." The foreign culture—particularly its emphasis on groups over individuals—was both a shock and a challenge to a young American woman. It wasn't just that she felt lonely in an alien world. She had to face the daunting prospect of carving out a place for herself as the only woman engineer in a plant, and nation, where women usually serve as low-level assistants and clerks known as "office ladies."

Another woman who had come to Japan under similar circumstances had warned Altman that the only way to win the men's respect was to avoid becoming allied with the office ladies. But on her very first morning, when the bell rang for a coffee break, the men headed in one direction and the women in another—and the women saved her a place at their table, while the men ignored her. Instinct told Altman to ignore the warning rather than insult the women by rebuffing their invitation.

Over the next few days, she continued to join the women during breaks, a choice that gave her a comfortable haven from which to observe the unfamiliar office culture. But it didn't take her long to notice that some of the men spent the break at their desks reading magazines, and Altman determined that she could do the same on occasion. Finally, after paying close attention to the conversations around her, she learned that several of the men were interested in mountain biking. Because Altman wanted to buy a mountain bike, she approached them for advice. Thus, over time, she established herself as something of a free agent, sometimes sitting with the women and other times engaging with the men.

And as it happened, one of the women she'd sat with on her very first day, the department secretary, was married to one of the engineers. The secretary took it upon herself to include Altman in social gatherings, a turn of events that probably wouldn't have occurred if Altman had alienated her female coworkers on that first day. "Had I just gone to try to break in with [the men] and not had her as an ally, it would never have happened," she says.

Looking back, Altman believes the experience greatly helped her gain a clearer sense of her personal strengths and capabilities, preparing her for other difficult situations. Her tenure in Japan taught her to observe closely and to avoid jumping to conclusions based on cultural assumptions—invaluable skills in her current position at Motorola, where she leads efforts to smooth alliances with other corporate cultures, including those of Motorola's different regional operations.

Altman has come to believe that she wouldn't have been as able to do the Motorola job if she hadn't lived in a foreign country and experienced the dissonance of cultures: ". . . even if you're sitting in the same room, ostensibly agreeing . . . unless you understand the frame of reference, you're probably missing a bunch of what's going on." Altman also credits her crucible with building her confidence—she feels that she can cope with just about anything that comes her way.

People can feel the stigma of cultural differences much closer to home, as well. Muriel ("Mickie") Siebert, the first woman to own a seat on the New York Stock Exchange, found her crucible on the Wall Street of the 1950s and 1960s, an arena so sexist that she couldn't get a job as a stockbroker until she took her first name off her résumé and substituted a genderless initial. Other than the secretaries and the occasional analyst, women were few and far between. That she was Jewish was another strike against her at a time, she points out, when most of big business was "not nice" to either women or Jews. But Siebert wasn't broken or defeated. Instead, she emerged stronger, more focused, and more determined to change the status quo that excluded her.

When we interviewed Siebert, she described her way of addressing anti-Semitism—a technique that quieted the offensive comments of her peers without destroying the relationships she needed to do her job effectively. According to Siebert, at the time it was part of doing business to have a few drinks at lunch. She remembers, "Give somebody a couple of drinks, and they would talk about the Jews." She had a greeting card she used for those occasions that went like this:

Roses are reddish,
Violets are bluish,
In case you don't know,
I am Jewish.

Siebert would have the card hand-delivered to the person who had made the anti-Semitic remarks, and on the card she had written, "Enjoyed lunch." As she recounts, "They got that card in the afternoon, and I never had to take any of that nonsense again. And I never embarrassed anyone, either." It was because she was unable to get credit for the business she was bringing in at any of the large Wall Street firms that she bought a seat on the New York Stock Exchange and started working for herself.

In subsequent years, she went on to found Muriel Siebert & Company (now Siebert Financial Corporation) and has dedicated herself to helping other people avoid some of the difficulties she faced as a young professional. A prominent advocate for women in business and a leader in developing financial products directed at women, she's also devoted to educating children about financial opportunities and responsibility.

We didn't interview lawyer and presidential adviser Vernon Jordan for this article, but he, too, offers a powerful reminder of how prejudice can prove transformational rather than debilitating. In *Vernon Can Read! A Memoir* (Public Affairs, 2001), Jordan describes the vicious baiting he was subjected to as a young man. The man who treated him in this offensive way was his employer, Robert F. Maddox. Jordan served the racist former mayor of Atlanta at dinner, in a white jacket, with a napkin over his arm. He also functioned as Maddox's chauffeur. Whenever Maddox could, he would derisively announce, "Vernon can read!" as if the literacy of a young African-American were a source of wonderment. Subjected to this type of abuse, a lesser man might have allowed Maddox to destroy him. But in his memoir, Jordan gives his own interpretation of Maddox's sadistic heckling, a tale that empowered Jordan instead of embittering him. When he looked at Maddox through the rearview mirror, Jordan did not see a powerful member of Georgia's ruling class. He saw a desperate anachronism, a person who lashed out because he knew his time was up. As Jordan writes about Maddox, "His half-mocking, half-serious comments about my education were the death rattle of his culture. When he saw that I was . . . crafting a life for myself that would make me a man in . . . ways he thought of as being a man, he was deeply unnerved."

Maddox's cruelty was the crucible that, consciously or not, Jordan imbued with redemptive meaning. Instead of lashing out or being paralyzed with hatred, Jordan saw the fall of the Old South and imagined his own future freed of the historical shackles of racism. His ability to organize meaning around a potential crisis turned it into the crucible around which his leadership was forged.

Prevailing over Darkness

Some crucible experiences illuminate a hidden and suppressed area of the soul. These are often among the harshest of crucibles, involving, for instance, episodes of illness or violence. In the case of Sidney Rittenberg, now 79, the crucible took the form of 16 years of unjust imprisonment, in solitary confinement, in Communist

China. In 1949 Rittenberg was initially jailed, without explanation, by former friends in Chairman Mao Zedong's government and spent his first year in total darkness when he wasn't being interrogated. (Rittenberg later learned that his arrest came at the behest of Communist Party officials in Moscow, who had wrongly identified him as a CIA agent.) Thrown into jail, confined to a tiny, pitch-dark cell, Rittenberg did not rail or panic. Instead, within minutes, he remembered a stanza of verse, four lines recited to him when he was a small child:

> *They drew a circle that shut me out,*
> *Heretic, rebel, a thing to flout.*
> *But love and I had the wit to win,*
> *We drew a circle that took them in!*

That bit of verse (adapted from "Outwitted," a poem by Edwin Markham) was the key to Rittenberg's survival. "My God," he thought, "there's my strategy." He drew the prison guards into his circle, developing relationships that would help him adapt to his confinement. Fluent in Chinese, he persuaded the guards to deliver him books and, eventually, provide a candle so that he could read. He also decided, after his first year, to devote himself to improving his mind—making it more scientific, more pure, and more dedicated to socialism. He believed that if he raised his consciousness, his captors would understand him better. And when, over time, the years in the dark began to take an intellectual toll on him and he found his reason faltering, he could still summon fairy tales and childhood stories such as *The Little Engine That Could* and take comfort from their simple messages.

By contrast, many of Rittenberg's fellow prisoners either lashed out in anger or withdrew. "They tended to go up the wall. . . . They couldn't make it. And I think the reason was that they didn't understand . . . that happiness . . . is not a function of your circumstances; it's a function of your outlook on life."

Rittenberg's commitment to his ideals continued upon his release. His cell door opened suddenly in 1955, after his first six-year term in prison. He recounts, "Here was a representative of the central government telling me that I had been wronged, that the government was making a formal apology to me . . . and that they would do everything possible to make restitution." When his captors offered him money to start a new life in the United States or to travel in Europe, Rittenberg declined, choosing instead to stay in China and continue his work for the Communist Party.

Fortunately, not all crucible experiences are traumatic. In fact, they can involve a positive, if deeply challenging, experience such as having a demanding boss or mentor.

And even after a second arrest, which put him into solitary confinement for ten years as retaliation for his support of open democracy during the Cultural Revolution, Rittenberg did not allow his spirit to be broken. Instead, he used his time in prison as an opportunity to question his belief system—in particular, his commitment to Marxism and Chairman Mao. "In that sense, prison emancipated me," he says.

Rittenberg studied, read, wrote, and thought, and he learned something about himself in the process: "I realized I had this great fear of being a turncoat, which . . . was so powerful that it prevented me from even looking at [my assumptions]. . . . Even to question was an act of betrayal. After I got out . . . the scales fell away from my eyes and I understood that . . . the basic doctrine of arriving at democracy through dictatorship was wrong."

What's more, Rittenberg emerged from prison certain that absolutely nothing in his professional life could break him and went on to start a company with his wife. Rittenberg Associates is a consulting firm dedicated to developing business ties between the United States and China. Today, Rittenberg is as committed to his ideals— if not to his view of the best way to get there—as he was 50 years ago, when he was so severely tested.

Meeting Great Expectations

Fortunately, not all crucible experiences are traumatic. In fact, they can involve a positive, if deeply challenging, experience such as having a demanding boss or mentor. Judge Nathaniel R. Jones of the U.S. Court of Appeals for the Sixth Circuit, for instance, attributes much of his success to his interaction with a splendid mentor. That mentor was J. Maynard Dickerson, a successful attorney—the first black city prosecutor in the United States—and editor of a local African-American newspaper.

Dickerson influenced Jones at many levels. For instance, the older man brought Jones behind the scenes to witness firsthand the great civil rights struggle of the 1950s, inviting him to sit in on conversations with activists like Thurgood Marshall, Walter White, Roy Wilkins, and Robert C. Weaver. Says Jones, "I was struck by their resolve, their humor . . . and their determination not to let the system define them. Rather than just feel beaten down, they turned it around." The experience no doubt influenced the many important opinions Judge Jones has written in regard to civil rights.

Dickerson was both model and coach. His lessons covered every aspect of Jones's intellectual growth and presentation of self, including schooling in what we now call "emotional intelligence." Dickerson set the highest

standards for Jones, especially in the area of communication skills—a facility we've found essential to leadership.
Dickerson edited Jones's early attempts at writing a
sports column with respectful ruthlessness, in red ink, as
Jones remembers to this day—marking up the copy so
that it looked, as Jones says, "like something chickens
had a fight over." But Dickerson also took the time to
explain every single mistake and why it mattered.

His mentor also expected the teenage Jones to speak
correctly at all times and would hiss discreetly in his
direction if he stumbled. Great expectations are evidence
of great respect, and as Jones learned all the complex,
often subtle lessons of how to succeed, he was motivated
in no small measure by his desire not to disappoint the
man he still calls "Mr. Dickerson." Dickerson gave Jones
the kind of intensive mentoring that was tantamount to
grooming him for a kind of professional and moral suc-
cession—and Jones has indeed become an instrument
for the profound societal change for which Dickerson
fought so courageously as well. Jones found life-changing
meaning in the attention Dickerson paid to him—attention fueled by a conviction that he, too, though only a
teenager, had a vital role to play in society and an important destiny.

Another story of a powerful mentor came to us from
Michael Klein, a young man who made millions in Southern California real estate while still in his teens, only to
lose it by the time he turned 20 and then go on to start
several other businesses. His mentor was his grandfather
Max S. Klein, who created the paint-by-numbers fad that
swept the United States in the 1950s and 1960s. Klein
was only four or five years old when his grandfather
approached him and offered to share his business expertise. Over the years, Michael Klein's grandfather taught

him to learn from and to cope with change, and the two spoke by phone for an hour every day until shortly before Max Klein's death.

The Essentials of Leadership

In our interviews, we heard many other stories of crucible experiences. Take Jack Coleman, 78-year-old former president of Haverford College in Pennsylvania. He told us of one day, during the Vietnam War, when he heard that a group of students was planning to pull down the American flag and burn it—and that former members of the school's football team were going to make sure the students didn't succeed. Seemingly out of nowhere, Coleman had the idea to preempt the violence by suggesting that the protesting students take down the flag, wash it, and then put it back up—a crucible moment that even now elicits tremendous emotion in Coleman as he describes that day.

There's also Common Cause founder John W. Gardner, who died earlier this year at 89. He identified his arduous training as a Marine during World War II as the crucible in which his leadership abilities emerged. Architect Frank Gehry spoke of the biases he experienced as a Jew in college. Jeff Wilke, a general manager at a major manufacturer, told us of the day he learned that an employee had been killed in his plant—an experience that taught him that leadership was about much more than making quarterly numbers.

So, what allowed these people to not only cope with these difficult situations but also learn from them? We believe that great leaders possess four essential skills, and, we were surprised to learn, these happen to be the same skills that allow a person to find meaning in what could be a debilitating experience. First is the ability to engage others in shared meaning. Consider Sidney Harman, who dived into a chaotic work environment to mobilize employees around an entirely new approach to management. Second is a distinctive and compelling voice. Look at Jack Coleman's ability to defuse a potentially violent situation with only his words. Third is a sense of integrity (including a strong set of values). Here, we point again to Coleman, whose values prevailed even during the emotionally charged clash between peace demonstrators and the angry (and strong) former football team members.

But by far the most critical skill of the four is what we call "adaptive capacity." This is, in essence, applied creativity—an almost magical ability to transcend adversity, with all its attendant stresses, and to emerge stronger than before. It's composed of two primary qualities: the ability to grasp context, and hardiness. The ability to grasp context implies an ability to weigh a welter of factors, ranging from how very different groups of people will interpret a gesture to being able to put a situation in perspective. Without this, leaders are utterly lost, because they cannot connect with their constituents. M. Douglas

It is the combination of hardiness and ability to grasp context that, above all, allows a person to not only survive an ordeal, but to learn from it, and to emerge stronger, more engaged, and more committed than ever.

Ivester, who succeeded Roberto Goizueta at Coca-Cola, exhibited a woeful inability to grasp context, lasting just 28 months on the job. For example, he demoted his highest-ranked African-American employee even as the company was losing a $200 million class-action suit brought by black employees—and this in Atlanta, a city with a powerful African-American majority. Contrast Ivester with Vernon Jordan. Jordan realized his boss's time was up—not just his time in power, but the era that formed him. And so Jordan was able to see past the insults and recognize his boss's bitterness for what it was—desperate lashing out.

Hardiness is just what it sounds like—the perseverance and toughness that enable people to emerge from devastating circumstances without losing hope. Look at Michael Klein, who experienced failure but didn't let it defeat him. He found himself with a single asset—a tiny software company he'd acquired. Klein built it into Transoft Networks, which Hewlett-Packard acquired in 1999. Consider, too, Mickie Siebert, who used her sense of humor to curtail offensive conversations. Or Sidney Rittenberg's strength during his imprisonment. He drew on his personal memories and inner strength to emerge from his lengthy prison term without bitterness.

It is the combination of hardiness and ability to grasp context that, above all, allows a person to not only survive an ordeal, but to learn from it, and to emerge stronger, more engaged, and more committed than ever. These attributes allow leaders to grow from their crucibles, instead of being destroyed by them—to find opportunity where others might find only despair. This is the stuff of true leadership.

Geeks and Geezers

WE DIDN'T SET OUT TO LEARN about crucibles. Our research for this article and for our new book, *Geeks and Geezers*, was actually designed to uncover the ways that era influences a leader's motivation and aspirations. We interviewed 43 of today's top leaders in business and the public sector, limiting our subjects to people born in or before 1925, or in or after 1970. To our delight, we learned a lot about how age and era affect leadership style.

Our geeks and geezers (the affectionate shorthand we eventually used to describe the two groups) had very different ideas about paying your dues, work-life balance, the role of heroes, and more. But they also shared some striking similarities—among them a love of learning and strong sense of values. Most intriguing, though, both our geeks and our geezers told us again and again how certain experiences inspired them, shaped them, and, indeed, taught them to lead. And so, as the best research often does, our work turned out to be even more interesting than we thought it would be. We continued to explore the influences of era—our findings are described in our book—but at the same time we probed for stories of these crucible experiences. These are the stories we share with you here.

Reinvention in the Extreme: The Power of Neoteny

ALL OF OUR INTERVIEW SUBJECTS described their crucibles as opportunities for reinvention—for taking stock of their lives and finding meaning in circumstances many people would see as daunting and potentially incapacitating. In the extreme, this capacity for reinvention comes to resemble eternal youth—a kind of vigor, openness, and an enduring capacity for wonder that is the antithesis of stereotyped old age.

We borrowed a term from biology—"neoteny," \
according to the *American Heritage Dictionary*, me
"retention of juvenile characteristics in the adults of a
species"—to describe this quality, this delight in lifelong
learning, which every leader we interviewed displayed,
regardless of age. To a person, they were full of energy,
curiosity, and confidence that the world is a place of
wonders spread before them like an endless feast.

Robert Galvin, former Motorola chairman now in his
late 70s, spends his weekends windsurfing. Arthur Levitt,
Jr., former SEC chairman who turned 71 this year, is an
avid Outward Bound trekker. And architect Frank Gehry is
now a 72-year-old ice hockey player. But it's not only an
affinity for physical activity that characterizes neoteny—it's
an appetite for learning and self-development, a curiosity
and passion for life.

To understand why this quality is so powerful in a
leader, it might help to take a quick look at the scientific
principle behind it—neoteny as an evolutionary engine. It
is the winning, puppyish quality of certain ancient wolves
that allowed them to evolve into dogs. Over thousands
of years, humans favored wolves that were the friendliest,
most approachable, and most curious. Naturally, people
were most drawn to the wolves least likely to attack without warning, that readily locked eyes with them, and that
seemed almost human in their eager response to people;
the ones, in short, that stayed the most like puppies. Like
human infants, they have certain physical qualities that
elicit a nurturing response in human adults.

When infants see an adult, they often respond with a
smile that begins small and slowly grows into a radiant
grin that makes the adult feel at center of the universe.
Recent studies of bonding indicate that nursing and other
intimate interactions with an infant cause the mother's

system to be flooded with oxytocin, a calming, feel-good hormone that is a powerful antidote to cortisol, the hormone produced by stress. Oxytocin appears to be the glue that produces bonding. And the baby's distinctive look and behaviors cause oxytocin to be released in the fortunate adult. That appearance—the one that pulls an involuntary "aaah" out of us whenever we see a baby— and those oxytocin-inducing behaviors allow infants to recruit adults to be their nurturers, essential if such vulnerable and incompletely developed creatures are to survive.

The power of neoteny to recruit protectors and nurturers was vividly illustrated in the former Soviet Union. Forty years ago, a Soviet scientist decided to start breeding silver foxes for neoteny at a Siberian fur farm. The goal was to create a tamer fox that would go with less fuss to slaughter than the typical silver fox. Only the least aggressive, most approachable animals were bred.

The experiment continued for 40 years, and today, after 35 generations, the farm is home to a breed of tame foxes that look and act more like juvenile foxes and even dogs than like their wild forebears. The physical changes in the animals are remarkable (some have floppy, dog-like ears), but what is truly stunning is the change neoteny has wrought in the human response to them. Instead of taking advantage of the fact that these neotenic animals don't snap and snarl on the way to their deaths, their human keepers appear to have been recruited by their newly cute and endearing charges. The keepers and the foxes appear to have formed close bonds, so close that the keepers are trying to find ways to save the animals from slaughter.

Originally published in September 2002
Reprint R0209B

A Survival Guide for Leaders

RONALD A. HEIFETZ AND MARTY LINSKY

Executive Summary

LET'S FACE IT, TO LEAD is to live dangerously. While
leadership is often viewed as an exciting and glamorous
endeavor, one in which you inspire others to follow you
through good times and bad, such a portrayal ignores
leadership's dark side: the inevitable attempts to take
you out of the game.

This is particularly true when a leader must steer an
organization through difficult change. When the status
quo is upset, people feel a sense of profound loss and
dashed expectations. They may need to undergo a
period of feeling incompetent or disloyal. It's no wonder
they resist the change and often try to eliminate its visible
agent.

This "survival guide" offers a number of techniques—
relatively straightforward in concept but difficult to
execute—for protecting yourself as you lead such a

change initiative. Adapted from the book *Leadership on the Line: Staying Alive Through the Dangers of Leading* (Harvard Business School Press, 2002), the article has two main parts. The first looks outward, offering tactical advice about relating to your organization and the people in it. It is designed to protect you from those who would push you aside before you complete your initiatives. The second looks inward, focusing on your own needs and vulnerabilities. It is designed to keep you from bringing yourself down.

The hard truth is it is not possible to experience the rewards and joys of leadership without experiencing the pain as well. But staying in the game and bearing that pain is worth it, not only for the positive changes you can make in the lives of others but also for the meaning it gives your own.

T HINK OF THE MANY TOP EXECUTIVES in recent years who, sometimes after long periods of considerable success, have crashed and burned. Or think of individuals you have known in less prominent positions, perhaps people spearheading significant change initiatives in their organizations, who have suddenly found themselves out of a job. Think about yourself: In exercising leadership, have *you* ever been removed or pushed aside?

Let's face it, to lead is to live dangerously. While leadership is often depicted as an exciting and glamorous endeavor, one in which you inspire others to follow you through good times and bad, such a portrayal ignores leadership's dark side: the inevitable attempts to take you out of the game.

Those attempts are sometimes justified. People in top positions must often pay the price for a flawed strategy or a series of bad decisions. But frequently, something more is at work. We're not talking here about conventional office politics; we're talking about the high-stake risks you face whenever you try to lead an organization through difficult but necessary change. The risks during such times are especially high because change that truly transforms an organization, be it a multibillion-dollar company or a ten-person sales team, demands that people give up things they hold dear: daily habits, loyalties, ways of thinking. In return for these sacrifices, they may be offered nothing more than the possibility of a better future.

We refer to this kind of wrenching organizational transformation as "adaptive change," something very different from the "technical change" that occupies people in positions of authority on a regular basis. Technical problems, while often challenging, can be solved applying existing know-how and the organization's current problem-solving processes. Adaptive problems resist these kinds of solutions because they require individuals throughout the organization to alter their ways; as the people themselves are the problem, the solution lies with them. (See "Adaptive Versus Technical Change: Whose Problem Is It?" at the end of this article.) Responding to an adaptive challenge with a technical fix may have some short-term appeal. But to make real progress, sooner or later those who lead must

Executives leading difficult change initiatives are often blissfully ignorant of an approaching threat until it is too late to respond.

ask themselves and the people in the organization to face a set of deeper issues—and to accept a solution that may require turning part or all of the organization upside down.

It is at this point that danger lurks. And most people who lead in such a situation—swept up in the action, championing a cause they believe in—are caught unawares. Over and over again, we have seen courageous souls blissfully ignorant of an approaching threat until it was too late to respond.

The hazard can take numerous forms. You may be attacked directly in an attempt to shift the debate to your character and style and avoid discussion of your initiative. You may be marginalized, forced into the position of becoming so identified with one issue that your broad authority is undermined. You may be seduced by your supporters and, fearful of losing their approval and affection, fail to demand they make the sacrifices needed for the initiative to succeed. You may be diverted from your goal by people overwhelming you with the day-to-day details of carrying it out, keeping you busy and preoccupied.

Each one of these thwarting tactics—whether done consciously or not—grows out of people's aversion to the organizational disequilibrium created by your initiative. By attempting to undercut you, people strive to restore order, maintain what is familiar to them, and protect themselves from the pains of adaptive change. They want to be comfortable again, and you're in the way.

So how do you protect yourself? Over a combined 50 years of teaching and consulting, we have asked ourselves that question time and again—usually while watching top-notch and well-intentioned folks get taken out of the game. On occasion, the question has become painfully personal; we as individuals have been knocked off course or out of the action more than once in our own leadership efforts. So we are offering what we hope are some pragmatic answers that grow out of these observations and experiences. We should note that while our advice clearly applies to senior executives, it also applies to people trying to lead change initiatives from positions of little or no formal organizational authority.

This "survival guide" has two main parts. The first looks outward, offering tactical advice about relating to your organization and the people in it. It is designed to protect you from those trying to push you aside before you complete your initiative. The second looks inward, focusing on your own human needs and vulnerabilities. It is designed to keep you from bringing yourself down.

A Hostile Environment

Leading major organizational change often involves radically reconfiguring a complex network of people, tasks, and institutions that have achieved a kind of modus vivendi, no matter how dysfunctional it appears to you. When the status quo is upset, people feel a sense of profound loss and dashed expectations. They may go through a period of feeling incompetent or disloyal. It's no wonder they resist the change or try to eliminate its visible agent. We offer here a number of techniques—relatively straightforward in concept but difficult to execute—for minimizing these external threats.

OPERATE IN AND ABOVE THE FRAY

The ability to maintain perspective in the midst of action is critical to lowering resistance. Any military officer knows the importance of maintaining the capacity for reflection, especially in the "fog of war." Great athletes must simultaneously play the game and observe it as a whole. We call this skill "getting off the dance floor and going to the balcony," an image that captures the mental activity of stepping back from the action and asking, "What's really going on here?"

Leadership is an improvisational art. You may be guided by an overarching vision, clear values, and a strategic plan, but what you actually do from moment to moment cannot be scripted. You must respond as events unfold. To use our metaphor, you have to move back and forth from the balcony to the dance floor, over and over again throughout the days, weeks, months, and years. While today's plan may make sense now, tomorrow you'll discover the unanticipated effects of today's actions and have to adjust accordingly. Sustaining good leadership, then, requires first and foremost the capacity to see what is happening to you and your initiative as it is happening and to understand how today's turns in the road will affect tomorrow's plans.

But taking a balcony perspective is extremely tough to do when you're fiercely engaged down below, being pushed and pulled by the events and people around you—and doing some pushing and pulling of your own. Even if you are able to break away, the practice of stepping back and seeing the big picture is complicated by several factors. For example, when you get some distance, you still must accurately interpret what you see and hear. This is easier said than done. In an attempt to avoid difficult change, people will naturally, even unconsciously, defend their habits and ways of thinking. As you seek input from a broad range of people, you'll constantly need to be aware of these hidden agendas. You'll also need to observe your own actions; seeing yourself objectively as you look down from the balcony is perhaps the hardest task of all.

Fortunately, you can learn to be both an observer and a participant at the same time. When you are sitting in a meeting, practice by watching what is happening while it is happening—even as you are part of what is happening. Observe the relationships and see how people's attention to one another can vary: supporting, thwarting, or listening. Watch people's body language. When you make a point, resist the instinct to stay perched on the edge of your seat, ready to defend what you said. A technique as simple as pushing your chair a few inches away from the table after you speak may provide the literal as well as metaphorical distance you need to become an observer.

COURT THE UNCOMMITTED

It's tempting to go it alone when leading a change initiative. There's no one to dilute your ideas or share the glory, and it's often just plain exciting. It's also foolish. You need to recruit partners, people who can help protect you from attacks and who can point out potentially fatal flaws in your strategy or initiative. Moreover, you are far less vulnerable when you are out on the point with a bunch of folks rather than alone. You also need to keep the opposition close. Knowing what your opponents are thinking can help you challenge them more effectively and thwart their attempts to upset your agenda—or allow you to borrow ideas that will improve your initiative. Have coffee once a week with the person most dedicated to seeing you fail.

But while relationships with allies and opponents are essential, the people who will determine your success are often those in the middle, the uncommitted who nonetheless are wary of your plans. They have no substantive stake in your initiative, but they do have a stake in the comfort, stability, and security of the status quo. They've seen change agents come and go, and they know that your initiative will disrupt their lives and make their futures uncertain. You want to be sure that this general uneasiness doesn't evolve into a move to push you aside.

These people will need to see that your intentions are serious—for example, that you are willing to let go of those who can't make the changes your initiative requires. But people must also see that you understand the loss you are asking them to accept. You need to name the loss, be it a change in time-honored work routines or an overhaul of the company's core values, and explicitly acknowledge the resulting pain. You might do this through a series of simple statements, but it often requires something more tangible and public—recall Franklin Roosevelt's radio "fireside chats" during the Great Depression—to convince people that you truly understand.

Beyond a willingness to accept casualties and acknowledge people's losses, two very personal types of action can defuse potential resistance to you and your initiatives. The first is practicing what you preach. In 1972, Gene Patterson took over as editor of the *St. Petersburg Times*. His mandate was to take the respected regional newspaper to a higher level, enhancing its reputation for fine writing while becoming a fearless and hard-hitting news source. This would require major changes not only in the way the community viewed the newspaper but also in the way *Times* reporters thought about themselves and their roles. Because prominent organizations and individuals would no longer be spared warranted criticism, reporters would sometimes be angrily rebuked by the subjects of articles.

Several years after Patterson arrived, he attended a party at the home of the paper's foreign editor. Driving home, he pulled up to a red light and scraped the car next to him. The police officer called to the scene charged Patterson with driving under the influence. Patterson phoned Bob Haiman, a veteran *Times* newsman who had just been appointed executive editor, and insisted that a story on his arrest be run. As Haiman recalls, he tried to talk Patterson out of it, arguing that DUI arrests that didn't involve injuries were rarely reported, even when prominent figures were involved. Patterson was adamant, however, and insisted that the story appear on page one.

Patterson, still viewed as somewhat of an outsider at the paper, knew that if he wanted his employees to follow the highest journalistic standards, he would have to display those standards, even when it hurt. Few leaders are called upon to disgrace themselves on the front page of a newspaper. But adopting the behavior you expect from others—whether it be taking a pay cut in tough times or spending a day working next to employees on a reconfigured production line—can be crucial in getting buy-in from people who might try to undermine your initiative.

To neutralize potential opposition, you should acknowledge your own responsibility for whatever problems the organization currently faces.

The second thing you can do to neutralize potential opposition is to acknowledge your own responsibility for whatever problems the organization currently faces. If you have been with the company for some time, whether in a position of senior authority or not, you've likely contributed in some way to the current mess. Even if you are

new, you need to identify areas of your own behavior
that could stifle the change you hope to make.

In our teaching, training, and consulting, we often ask
people to write or talk about a leadership challenge they
currently face. Over the years, we have read and heard
literally thousands of such challenges. Typically, in the
first version of the story, the author is nowhere to be
found. The underlying message: "If only other people
would shape up, I could make progress here." But by too
readily pointing your finger at others, you risk making
yourself a target. Remember, you are asking people to
move to a place where they are frightened to go. If at the
same time you're blaming them for having to go there,
they will undoubtedly turn against you.

In the early 1990s, Leslie Wexner, founder and CEO of
the Limited, realized the need for major changes at the
company, including a significant reduction in the workforce. But his consultant told him that something else
had to change: long-standing habits that were at the
heart of his self-image. In particular, he had to stop treating the company as if it were his family. The indulgent
father had to become the chief personnel officer, putting
the right people in the right jobs and holding them
accountable for their work. "I was an athlete trained to
be a baseball player," Wexner recalled during a recent
speech at Harvard's Kennedy School. "And one day,
someone tapped me on the shoulder and said, 'Football.'
And I said, 'No, I'm a baseball player.' And he said, 'Football.' And I said, 'I don't know how to play football. I'm
not 6'4", and I don't weigh 300 pounds.' But if no one values baseball anymore, the baseball player will be out of
business. So I looked into the mirror and said, 'Schlemiel,
nobody wants to watch baseball. Make the transformation to football.'" His personal makeover—shedding the
role of forgiving father to those widely viewed as not

holding their own—helped sway other employees to back a corporate makeover. And his willingness to change helped protect him from attack during the company's long—and generally successful—turnaround period.

COOK THE CONFLICT

Managing conflict is one of the greatest challenges a leader of organizational change faces. The conflict may involve resistance to change, or it may involve clashing viewpoints about how the change should be carried out. Often, it will be latent rather than palpable. That's because most organizations are allergic to conflict, seeing it primarily as a source of danger, which it certainly can be. But conflict is a necessary part of the change process and, if handled properly, can serve as the engine of progress.

Thus, a key imperative for a leader trying to achieve significant change is to manage people's passionate differences in a way that diminishes their destructive potential and constructively harnesses their energy. Two techniques can help you achieve this. First, create a secure place where the conflicts can freely bubble up. Second, control the temperature to ensure that the conflict doesn't boil over—and burn you in the process.

The vessel in which a conflict is simmered—in which clashing points of view mix, lose some of their sharpness, and ideally blend into consensus—will look and feel quite different in different contexts. It may be a protected physical space, perhaps an off-site location where an outside facilitator helps a group work through its differences. It may be a clear set of rules and processes that give minority voices confidence that they will be heard without having to disrupt the proceedings to gain attention. It may be the shared language and history of an organization that binds people together through trying times. Whatever its form, it is a place or a means to contain the roiling forces unleashed by the threat of major change.

But a vessel can withstand only so much strain before it blows. A huge challenge you face as a leader is keeping your employees' stress at a productive level. The success of the change effort—as well as your own authority and even survival—requires you to monitor your organization's tolerance for heat and then regulate the temperature accordingly.

You first need to raise the heat enough that people sit up, pay attention, and deal with the real threats and challenges facing them. After all, without some distress, there's no incentive to change. You can constructively raise the temperature by focusing people's attention on the hard issues, by forcing them to take responsibility for tackling and solving those issues, and by bringing conflicts occurring behind closed doors out into the open.

But you have to lower the temperature when necessary to reduce what can be counterproductive turmoil. You can turn down the heat by slowing the pace of change or by tackling some relatively straightforward technical aspect of the problem, thereby reducing people's anxiety levels and allowing them to get warmed up for bigger challenges. You can provide structure to the problem-solving process, creating work groups with specific assignments, setting time parameters, establishing rules for decision making, and outlining reporting relationships. You can use humor or find an excuse for a break or a party to temporarily ease tensions. You can speak to people's fears and, more critically, to their hopes for a more promising future. By showing people how the future might look, you come to embody hope rather than fear, and you reduce the likelihood of becoming a lightning rod for the conflict.

The aim of both these tactics is to keep the heat high enough to motivate people but low enough to prevent a disastrous explosion—what we call a "productive range of distress." Remember, though, that most employees will reflexively want you to turn down the heat; their complaints may in fact indicate that the environment is just right for hard work to get done.

We've already mentioned a classic example of managing the distress of fundamental change: Franklin Roosevelt during the first few years of his presidency. When he took office in 1933, the chaos, tension, and anxiety brought on by the Depression ran extremely high. Demagogues stoked class, ethnic, and racial conflict that threatened to tear the nation apart. Individuals feared an uncertain future. So Roosevelt first did what he could to reduce the sense of disorder to a tolerable level. He took decisive and authoritative action—he pushed an extraordinary number of bills through Congress during his fabled first 100 days—and thereby gave Americans a sense of direction and safety, reassuring them that they were in capable hands. In his fireside chats, he spoke to people's anxiety and anger and laid out a positive vision for the future that made the stress of the current crisis bearable and seem a worthwhile price to pay for progress.

But he knew the problems facing the nation couldn't be solved from the White House. He needed to mobilize citizens and get them to dream up, try out, fight over, and ultimately own the sometimes painful solutions that would transform the country and move it forward. To do that, he needed to maintain a certain level of fermentation and distress. So, for example, he orchestrated conflicts over public priorities and programs among the large cast of creative people he brought into the government. By giving the same assignment to two different administrators and refusing to clearly define their roles, he got them to generate new and competing ideas. Roosevelt displayed both the acuity to recognize when the tension in the nation had risen too high and the emotional strength to take the heat and permit considerable anxiety to persist.

PLACE THE WORK WHERE IT BELONGS

Because major change requires people across an entire organization to adapt, you as a leader need to resist the reflex reaction of providing people with the answers. Instead, force yourself to transfer, as Roosevelt did, much of the work and problem solving to others. If you don't, real and sustainable change won't occur. In addition, it's risky on a personal level to continue to hold on to the work that should be done by others.

As a successful executive, you have gained credibility and authority by demonstrating your capacity to solve other people's problems. This ability can be a virtue, until you find yourself faced with a situation in which you cannot deliver solutions. When this happens, all of your habits, pride, and sense of competence get thrown out of kilter because you must mobilize the work of others rather than find the way yourself. By trying to solve an adaptive challenge for people, at best you will reconfigure it as a technical problem and create some short-term relief. But the issue will not have gone away.

In the 1994 National Basketball Association Eastern Conference semifinals, the Chicago Bulls lost to the New York Knicks in the first two games of the best-of-seven series. Chicago was out to prove that it was more than just a one-man team, that it could win without Michael Jordan, who had retired at the end of the previous season.

In the third game, the score was tied at 102 with less than two seconds left. Chicago had the ball and a time-out to plan a final shot. Coach Phil Jackson called for Scottie Pippen, the Bulls' star since Jordan had retired, to make the inbound pass to Toni Kukoc for the final shot. As play was about to resume, Jackson noticed Pippen sitting at the far end of the bench. Jackson asked him whether he was in or out. "I'm out," said Pippen, miffed that he was not tapped to take the final shot. With only four players on the floor, Jackson quickly called another time-out and substituted an excellent passer, the reserve Pete Myers, for Pippen. Myers tossed a perfect pass to Kukoc, who spun around and sank a miraculous shot to win the game.

The Bulls made their way back to the locker room, their euphoria deflated by Pippen's extraordinary act of insubordination. Jackson recalls that as he entered a silent room, he was uncertain about what to do. Should he punish Pippen? Make him apologize? Pretend the whole thing never happened? All eyes were on him. The coach looked around, meeting the gaze of each player, and said, "What happened has hurt us. Now you have to work this out."

Jackson knew that if he took action to resolve the immediate crisis, he would have made Pippen's behavior a matter between coach and player. But he understood that a deeper issue was at the heart of the incident: Who were the Chicago Bulls without Michael Jordan? It wasn't about who was going to succeed Jordan, because no one was; it was about whether the players could jell as a team where no one person dominated and every player was willing to do whatever it took to help. The issue rested with the players, not him, and only they could resolve it. It did not matter what they decided at that moment; what mattered was that they, not Jackson, did the deciding. What followed was a discussion led by an emotional Bill Cartwright, a team veteran. According to Jackson, the conversation brought the team closer together. The Bulls took the series to a seventh game before succumbing to the Knicks.

Jackson gave the work of addressing both the Pippen and the Jordan issues back to the team for another reason: If he had taken ownership of the problem, he would have become the issue, at least for the moment. In his case, his position as coach probably wouldn't have been threatened. But in other situations, taking responsibility for resolving a conflict within the organization poses risks. You are likely to find yourself resented by the faction that you decide against and held responsible by nearly everyone for the turmoil your decision generates. In the eyes of many, the only way to neutralize the threat is to get rid of you.

Despite that risk, most executives can't resist the temptation to solve fundamental organizational problems by themselves. People expect you to get right in there and fix things, to take a stand and resolve the problem. After all, that is what top managers are paid to do. When you fulfill those expectations, people will call you admirable and courageous—even a "leader"—and that is flattering. But challenging your employees' expectations requires greater courage and leadership.

The Dangers Within

We have described a handful of leadership tactics you can use to interact with the people around you, particularly those who might undermine your initiatives. Those tactics can help advance your initiatives and, just as important, ensure that you remain in a position where you can bring them to fruition. But from our own observations and painful personal experiences, we know that one of the surest ways for an organization to bring you down is simply to let you precipitate your own demise. In the heat of leadership, with the adrenaline pumping, it is easy to convince yourself that you are not subject to the normal human frailties that can defeat ordinary mortals. You begin to act as if you are indestructible. But the intellectual, physical, and emotional challenges of leadership are fierce. So, in addition to getting on the balcony, you need to regularly step into the inner chamber of your being and assess the tolls those challenges are taking. If you don't, your seemingly indestructible self can self-destruct. This, by the way, is an ideal outcome for your foes—and even friends who oppose your initiative—because no one has to feel responsible for your downfall.

MANAGE YOUR HUNGERS

We all have hungers, expressions of our normal human needs. But sometimes those hungers disrupt our capacity to act wisely or purposefully. Whether inherited or products of our upbringing, some of these hungers may be so strong that they render us constantly vulnerable. More typically, a stressful situation or setting can exaggerate a normal level of need, amplifying our desires and overwhelming our usual self-discipline. Two of the most common and dangerous hungers are the desire for control and the desire for importance.

Everyone wants to have some measure of control over his or her life. Yet some people's need for control is disproportionately high. They might have grown up in a household that was either tightly structured or unusually chaotic; in either case, the situation drove them to become masters at taming chaos not only in their own lives but also in their organizations.

That need for control can be a source of vulnerability. Initially, of course, the ability to turn disorder into order may be seen as an attribute. In an organization facing turmoil, you may seem like a godsend if you are able (and desperately want) to step in and take charge. By lowering the distress to a tolerable level, you keep the kettle from boiling over.

But in your desire for order, you can mistake the means for the end. Rather than ensuring that the distress level in an organization remains high enough to mobilize progress on the issues, you focus on maintaining order as an end in itself. Forcing people to make the difficult trade-offs required by fundamental change threatens a return to the disorder you loathe. Your ability to bring the situation under control also suits the people in the organization, who naturally prefer calm to chaos. Unfortunately, this desire for control makes you vulnerable to, and an agent of, the organization's wish to avoid working through contentious issues. While this may ensure your survival in the short term, ultimately you may find yourself accused, justifiably, of failing to deal with the tough challenges when there was still time to do so.

Most people also have some need to feel important and affirmed by others. The danger here is that you will let this affirmation give you an inflated view of yourself and your cause. A grandiose sense of self-importance often leads to self-deception. In particular, you tend to forget the creative role that doubt—which reveals parts of reality that you wouldn't otherwise see—plays in getting your organization to improve. The absence of doubt leads you to see only that which confirms your own competence, which will virtually guarantee disastrous missteps.

Another harmful side effect of an inflated sense of self-importance is that you will encourage people in the organization to become dependent on you. The higher the level of distress, the greater their hopes and expectations that you will provide deliverance. This relieves them of any responsibility for moving the organization forward. But their dependence can be detrimental not only to the group but to you personally. Dependence can quickly turn to contempt as your constituents discover your human shortcomings.

Two well-known stories from the computer industry illustrate the perils of dependency—and how to avoid them. Ken Olsen, the founder of Digital Equipment Corporation, built the company into a 120,000-person operation that, at its peak, was the chief rival of IBM. A generous man, he treated his employees extraordinarily well and experimented with personnel policies designed to increase the creativity, teamwork, and satisfaction of his workforce. This, in tandem with the company's success over the years, led the company's top management to turn to him as the sole decision maker on all key issues. His decision to shun the personal computer market because of his belief that few people would ever want to own a PC, which seemed reasonable

To survive, you need a sanctuary where you can reflect on the previous day's journey, renew your emotional resources, and recalibrate your moral compass.

at the time, is generally viewed as the beginning of the end for the company. But that isn't the point; everyone in business makes bad decisions. The point is, Olsen had fostered such an atmosphere of dependence that his decisions were rarely challenged by colleagues—at least not until it was too late.

Contrast that decision with Bill Gates's decision some years later to keep Microsoft out of the Internet business. It didn't take long for him to reverse his stand and launch a corporate overhaul that had Microsoft's delivery of Internet services as its centerpiece. After watching the rapidly changing computer industry and listening carefully to colleagues, Gates changed his mind with no permanent damage to his sense of pride and an enhanced reputation due to his nimble change of course.

ANCHOR YOURSELF

To survive the turbulent seas of a change initiative, you need to find ways to steady and stabilize yourself. First, you must establish a safe harbor where each day you can reflect on the previous day's journey, repair the psychological damage you have incurred, renew your stores of emotional resources, and recalibrate your moral compass. Your haven might be a physical place, such as the kitchen table of a friend's house, or a regular routine, such as a daily walk through the neighborhood. Whatever the sanctuary, you need to use and protect it. Unfortunately, seeking such respite is often seen as a luxury, making it one of the first things to go when life gets stressful and you become pressed for time.

Second, you need a confidant, someone you can talk to about what's in your heart and on your mind without

fear of being judged or betrayed. Once the undigested
mess is on the table, you can begin to separate, with your
confidant's honest input, what is worthwhile from
what is simply venting. The confidant, typically not a
coworker, can also pump you up when you're down and
pull you back to earth when you start taking praise too
seriously. But don't confuse confidants with allies:
Instead of supporting your current initiative, a confidant
simply supports you. A common mistake is to seek a
confidant among trusted allies, whose personal loyalty
may evaporate when a new issue more important to
them than you begins to emerge and take center stage.

Perhaps most important, you need to distinguish
between your personal self, which can serve as an anchor
in stormy weather, and your professional role, which
never will. It is easy to mix up the two. And other people
only increase the confusion: Colleagues, subordinates,
and even bosses often act as if the role you play is the
real you. But that is not the case, no matter how much of
yourself—your passions, your values, your talents—you
genuinely and laudably pour into your professional role.
Ask anyone who has experienced the rude awakening
that comes when they leave a position of authority and
suddenly find that their phone calls aren't returned as
quickly as they used to be.

That harsh lesson holds another important truth that
is easily forgotten: When people attack someone in a
position of authority, more often than not they are attacking the role, not the person. Even when attacks on you
are highly personal, you need to read them primarily as
reactions to how you, in your role, are affecting people's
lives. Understanding the criticism for what it is prevents it
from undermining your stability and sense of self-worth.
And that's important because when you feel the sting of

an attack, you are likely to become defensive and lash out at your critics, which can precipitate your downfall.

We hasten to add that criticism may contain legitimate points about how you are performing your role. For example, you may have been tactless in raising an issue with your organization, or you may have turned the heat up too quickly on a change initiative. But, at its heart, the criticism is usually about the issue, not you. Through the guise of attacking you personally, people often are simply trying to neutralize the threat they perceive in your point of view. Does anyone ever attack you when you hand out big checks or deliver good news? People attack your personality, style, or judgment when they don't like the message.

When you take "personal" attacks personally, you unwittingly conspire in one of the common ways you can be taken out of action—you make yourself the issue. Contrast the manner in which presidential candidates Gary Hart and Bill Clinton handled charges of philandering. Hart angrily counterattacked, criticizing the scruples of the reporters who had shadowed him. This defensive personal response kept the focus on his behavior. Clinton, on national television, essentially admitted he had strayed, acknowledging his piece of the mess. His strategic handling of the situation allowed him to return the campaign's focus to policy issues. Though both attacks were extremely personal, only Clinton understood that they were basically attacks on positions he represented and the role he was seeking to play.

Do not underestimate the difficulty of distinguishing self from role and responding coolly to what feels like a personal attack—particularly when the criticism comes, as it will, from people you care about. But disciplining yourself to do so can provide you with an anchor that will keep you from running aground and give you the stability to remain calm, focused, and persistent in engaging people with the tough issues.

Why Lead?

We will have failed if this "survival manual" for avoiding the perils of leadership causes you to become cynical or callous in your leadership effort or to shun the challenges of leadership altogether. We haven't touched on the thrill of inspiring people to come up with creative solutions that can transform an organization for the better. We hope we have shown that the essence of leadership lies in the capacity to deliver disturbing news and raise difficult questions in a way that moves people to take up the message rather than kill the messenger. But we haven't talked about the reasons that someone might want to take these risks.

Of course, many people who strive for high-authority positions are attracted to power. But in the end, that isn't enough to make the high stakes of the game worthwhile. We would argue that, when they look deep within themselves, people grapple with the challenges of leadership in order to make a positive difference in the lives of others.

When corporate presidents and vice presidents reach their late fifties, they often look back on careers devoted to winning in the marketplace. They may have succeeded remarkably, yet some people have difficulty making sense of their lives in light of what they have given up. For too many, their accomplishments seem empty. They question whether they should have been more aggressive in questioning corporate purposes or creating more ambitious visions for their companies.

Our underlying assumption in this article is that you can lead *and* stay alive—not just register a pulse, but really be alive. But the classic protective devices of a person in authority tend to insulate them from those qualities that foster an acute experience of living. Cynicism, often dressed up as realism, undermines creativity and daring. Arrogance, often posing as authoritative knowledge, snuffs out curiosity and the eagerness to question. Callousness, sometimes portrayed as the thick skin of experience, shuts out compassion for others.

The hard truth is that it is not possible to know the rewards and joys of leadership without experiencing the pain as well. But staying in the game and bearing that pain is worth it, not only for the positive changes you can make in the lives of others but also for the meaning it gives your own.

Adaptive Versus Technical Change: Whose Problem Is It?

THE IMPORTANCE—AND DIFFICULTY—of distinguishing between adaptive and technical change can be illustrated with an analogy. When your car has problems, you go to a mechanic. Most of the time, the mechanic can fix the car. But if your car troubles stem from the way a family member drives, the problems are likely to recur. Treating the problems as purely technical ones—taking the car to the mechanic time and again to get it back on the road—masks the real issues. Maybe you need to get your mother to stop drinking and driving, get your grandfather to give up his driver's license, or get your teenager to be more cautious. Whatever the underlying problems, the mechanic can't solve them. Instead, changes in the family need to occur, and that won't be easy. People will resist the moves, even denying that such problems exist. That's because even those not directly affected by an adaptive change typically experience discomfort when someone upsets a group's or an organization's equilibrium.

Such resistance to adaptive change certainly happens in business. Indeed, it's the classic error: Companies treat adaptive challenges as if they were technical problems. For example, executives attempt to improve the bottom line by cutting costs across the board. Not only does this avoid the need to make tough choices about which areas should be trimmed, it also masks the fact that the company's real challenge lies in redesigning its strategy.

Treating adaptive challenges as technical ones permits executives to do what they have excelled at throughout their careers: solve other people's problems. And it allows others in the organization to enjoy the primordial peace of mind that comes from knowing that their commanding officer has a plan to maintain order and stability. After all, the executive doesn't have to instigate—and the people don't have to undergo—uncomfortable change. Most people would agree that, despite the selective pain of a cost-cutting exercise, it is less traumatic than reinventing a company.

Originally published in June 2002
Reprint R0206C

The Toxic Handler

Organizational Hero—and Casualty

PETER FROST AND SANDRA ROBINSON

Executive Summary

YOU'VE WATCHED THEM COMFORT colleagues, defuse tense situations, and take the heat from tough bosses. You've seen them step in to ease the pain during layoffs and change programs. Who are they? The authors call them *toxic handlers*—managers who voluntarily shoulder the sadness, frustration, bitterness, and anger of others so that high-quality work continues to get done.

Toxic handlers are not new. They are probably as old as organizations themselves. But there has never been a systematic study of the role they play in business. In this article, the authors introduce the role of toxic handlers, explaining what they do and why.

Managing the pain of others is hard work. Toxic handlers save organizations from self-destructing, but they often pay a high price—emotionally, professionally, and sometimes physically. Some toxic handlers

experience burnout; others suffer far worse consequences, such as ulcers and heart attacks.

The authors contend that these unsung corporate
heroes have strategic importance in today's business
environment. Effective pain management can—and does—
contribute to the bottom line. No company can afford to
let talented employees burn out. Nor can it afford to
have a reputation as an unhappy place to work. The
authors offer practical advice for managers and organizations about how to support toxic handlers—before a
crisis strikes. The role of the toxic handler needs to be
given the attention it deserves for everyone's benefit,
because the health of employees is a key element in the
long-term competitiveness of companies and of society.

As a senior project manager at a public utility
company, Michael had thrived in his job for nearly a
decade. His team of 24 engineers worked quickly and
effectively together and was often the source of creative
ideas that helped the rest of the organization. All that
changed, however, when the utility's board brought in a
hard-charging CEO and made Michael one of his direct
reports. "He walked all over people," Michael recalls. "He
made fun of them; he intimidated them. He criticized
work for no reason, and he changed his plans daily.
Another project manager was hospitalized with ulcers
and took early retirement. People throughout the organization felt scared and betrayed. Everyone was running
around and whispering, and the copy machine was going
nonstop with résumés. No one was working. People
could barely function."

Rather than watch the organization come to a standstill, Michael stepped between the new CEO and his colleagues. He allowed people to vent their frustrations to him behind closed doors and even cry or shout. At meetings, when the CEO picked on coworkers, Michael stood up for them—and often ended up taking verbal beatings. He also played the role of the CEO's front man, translating his seemingly irrational directives so that people could put them into action. "He's not such a bad guy," was Michael's common refrain. "Underneath it all, he wants the best for the company."

Michael kept at it for three years, until the board fired the CEO. By then, however, Michael was considering leaving not just the company but his profession. "I didn't know if I could take the heat in a large organization anymore," he says. "In the end, I stayed with the company, but I took a year off from being a manager and just worked with the team. I had to recharge."

Toxic handlers voluntarily shoulder the sadness and the anger that are endemic to organizational life.

Take the heat—that's how Michael describes his role of absorbing and softening the emotional pain of his organization. It was a critical role, too. After the bad-tempered CEO was gone, members of Michael's team told the board that they had kept at their work largely because of Michael's soothing words, compassionate listening, and protection.

Michael is what we call a *toxic handler*, a manager who voluntarily shoulders the sadness, frustration, bitterness, and anger that are endemic to organizational life. Although toxic handlers may be found at every level in organizations, many work near the top—they run the marketing or new-product development department, for instance, or oversee several cross-functional teams. Virtually all of them carry a full load of "regular" work, and do so very well. In fact, it is often their superior performance that affords them the job security to play the role of toxic handler in the first place.

Toxic handlers are not new. They are probably as old as organizations, for organizations have always generated distress, just as they have always generated feelings of joy and fulfillment. Strong emotions are part of life; they are part of business. And yet there has never been a systematic study of the role toxic handlers play in business organizations. For the past two years, they have been at the center of our research: we have interviewed and observed about 70 executives who are either toxic handlers themselves or have managed people in the role. Our goal has been to understand what toxic handlers do, why they do it, and how organizations can support them.

Research on topics such as organizational pain is sometimes derided for being soft or unrealistic or even for being "politically correct." "Those people," the criticism goes, "don't understand how real organizations work. Companies can't be bothered with making everyone feel warm and fuzzy. There's a bottom line to worry about." But our study did not start with an assumption that organizations, per se, are responsible for their employees' personal happiness. Rather, we were motivated to study toxic handlers because of their strategic importance in today's business environment.

Success is a function of great ideas. But great ideas dry up when people are hurting or focused on organizational dysfunction.

In our current market-based and knowledge-driven world, success is a function of great ideas, which, of course, spring from intelligent, energized, and emotionally involved people. But great ideas dry up when people are hurting or when they are focused on organizational dysfunction. It is toxic handlers who frequently step in and absorb others' pain so that high-quality work continues to get done. For that reason alone, understanding toxic handlers is essential: to miss their contribution, or to underestimate it, is to neglect a powerful source of organizational effectiveness.

The contribution of toxic handlers merits attention for another critical reason. Organizations must recognize the toxic handlers in their midst so that their important work can be supported before a crisis strikes. Because although toxic handlers save organizations from self-destructing, they often pay a steep price—professionally, psychologically, and sometimes physically. Some toxic handlers experience burnout; others suffer from far worse, such as ulcers and heart attacks.

What Toxic Handlers Do

To illustrate the varied tasks toxic handlers take on, consider Alexandra, a vice president at a large financial institution in New York. Technically speaking, Alexandra was responsible for commercial and small-business accounts, but in reality she spent at least half of her time counseling coworkers. For instance, she frequently played peacemaker between the bank's large administrative staff and its constant stream of new M.B.A.'s.

"They always came in acting like they owned the world. Let's just say they tended to be pretty arrogant and heavy-handed with the secretaries and clerical workers," Alexandra recalls. "They offended them so much that they couldn't concentrate on their work. So first I had to explain to the staff that these young professionals were really good people inside, just seriously lacking in interpersonal skills. Then I had to pull the new M.B.A.'s into my office and help them understand that being a boss didn't mean bossing people around. And I had to do that without getting their backs up, otherwise they would have panicked, and that would have killed productivity. It was incredibly delicate stuff.

"I also spent hours on end talking other managers through their fears and insecurities around our possible merger with another bank," Alexandra says. "It was in the newspaper regularly, and people would come running to my office. Everyone was terrified they were going to get fired. One by one, I would calm everybody down so they could get back to their real jobs."

In general, then, toxic handlers alleviate organizational pain in five ways:

They listen empathetically. When staff members burst into his office on fire with anger and frustration, Michael, the project manager in our first example, almost always pointed them toward a chair while he closed the door. At that point, he would let them cool down without interruption. "I didn't say much," Michael recalls. "But I would look them in the eye and do a lot of nodding." Toxic handlers are experts at such nonjudgmental, compassionate listening.

They suggest solutions. Toxic handlers don't just listen, however, they also solve problems. Alexandra actively counseled staff members on how to speak with M.B.A.'s to avoid confrontations, and she similarly schooled M.B.A.'s in office etiquette. She often

advised secretaries, for instance, to meet with the
M.B.A.'s early in their tenures to lay out explicit
ground rules for communication.

They work behind the scenes to prevent pain. When
toxic handlers see a surefire case of organizational
pain on the horizon, they typically leap into action to
douse it. Consider the case of a talented employee
who had lost her self-confidence working for a difficult boss and was bound to be transferred, against her
wishes, to another department. Working without the
knowledge of the unhappy employee, a toxic handler
in the organization negotiated for weeks to move the
woman to a department known for its upbeat boss
and interesting work. The toxic handler commented
later, "The whole thing had to be done very tactfully
and with political sensitivity, including getting buy-in
from the HR department, or the woman would have
been labeled a whiner and a loser, and I would have
been accused by her boss of meddling. In the end,
everyone won." The woman, interestingly, never
learned the story behind her transfer.

They carry the confidences of others. Toxic handlers
can be like priests. In hearing and keeping secrets
well, they allow their coworkers to walk away less
troubled. Alexandra let her colleagues off-load their
fears about the bank's merger onto her, and they
returned to their jobs renewed. Similarly, Alan, a
human resources manager at an insurance company,
frequently listened to anguished colleagues who were
preparing to fire someone. On one occasion, the CEO
confided to him that a major layoff was in the works.
Later, Alan found out he was the only one in the organization who knew beforehand. The CEO told him, "I

had to proceed with the layoff decision, regardless of how much I might have felt for those let go. Sharing the news with you gave me some comfort."

They reframe difficult messages. Like Michael, who occasionally served as the abusive CEO's front man, toxic handlers act as diplomats and organizational translators. Alexandra heard staff members screaming about obnoxious new M.B.A.'s, but she delivered the message in language they could accept. "A company is like a small town," she often began, "where a bad reputation is hard to lose."

Another toxic handler was told by his boss, "Tell those idiots out there to get their act together and finish the job by Friday or else they're all doomed." The manager pulled his staff together and put the directive as such: "The boss needs us to complete this task by Friday, so let's put our heads together and see what we need to do to meet this deadline." By taking the sting out, the toxic handler allowed his staff to focus on the challenge of the directive without seeing it as an attack on their capabilities. The pain was managed, and the job got done.

Filling a Need

Toxic handlers are not new, but our research strongly suggests that two trends in recent years have intensified the need for them. Foremost among them is the growing prevalence of change initiatives. Pursuing the mantra that nonstop change is not just good, it's downright essential, many executives have spent the past decade reengineering, restructuring, and reinventing their organizations. In many cases, such transformations have created enormous shareholder value. Invariably, they have also caused confusion, fear, and anguish among employees. Downsizing is the other trend that has increased the need for toxic handlers. Whenever a company lays off employees, the people left behind feel a backwash of guilt and fear. As the question "Who will be next?" swirls around the organization, toxic handlers step in to soothe nerves and redirect people's energies back to work.

Although change and downsizing have increased in recent years, some types of organizational pain have always been—and will always be—with us. For instance, every organization experiences bursts of incidental distress: a beloved manager dies in a plane crash, a major division faces an unexpected broadside from an upstart competitor, or senior managers simply do something unwise. Take the case of Rick, a human resources manager who was asked to implement a new policy of promotions based on performance rather than seniority. At first, the policy was strongly supported by the CEO and his team, but once it went into action, old colleagues lobbied them hard, and they quickly backed down. Younger employees who supported the new policy felt betrayed, and they clamored for the CEO and his team to stand firm. Rick was caught in the middle of this managerial muddle and, for several weeks, he heard fervent outpourings from both sides. His toxic-handling role ended two months later when the CEO announced that he would abandon the revamped policy. Not everyone was happy, but as the confusion dissipated, so, too, did the worst of the organizational pain.

By contrast, some organizational pain is chronic: the organizations themselves are toxic, systematically generating distress through policies and practices. The most common of these are unreasonable stretch goals or performance targets, but toxicity is also created by unrelenting internal competition—toxic organizations love "horse races." Moreover, organizations that are chronically toxic are usually characterized by cultures of blame and dishonesty. No one takes responsibility for mistakes. In fact, people work assiduously to cover them up.

The final reason that toxic handlers exist is because the business world has toxic bosses. People like the CEO in our first story create organizational pain through insensitivity or vindictive behavior. Other toxic bosses cause pain because they are unwilling to take on the responsibilities of leadership, leaving subordinates hanging, confused, or paralyzed—or all three. Still others are toxic because of their extraordinarily high need for control, looking over the shoulders of people who have a job to do. Finally, some toxic bosses are unethical, creating conditions that compromise their colleagues and subordinates.

Toxic bosses very often work in tandem with a toxic handler. That's not surprising, since toxic bosses without handlers can be found out and then may face censure or even be fired. (It is worth noting that many toxic bosses are highly adept at managing their own bosses.) In one case we studied, a toxic boss had brought his chief lieutenant—his toxic handler—with him from one job to another for 15 years. The toxic handler routinely filtered the toxic boss's anger and prevented chaos. After meetings filled with belligerent tirades, for instance, the toxic handler would walk from office to office, explaining the boss's "real" opinions and assuring people he was not as angry as he seemed. And so the organizations they worked for continued to function. (To understand why toxic handlers do it, see "More Than a Job" at the end of this article.)

The Toll of Toxic Handling

Managing organizational pain is vital to the health of the enterprise—but at great cost to the health of the toxic handlers themselves. The negative repercussions of toxic handling are particularly high when the role is played for too long or when there is no letup in the stream of emotional problems to which they are exposed, as is the case in companies with chronic toxicity.

The most common toll of toxic handling—whatever its cause—is burnout, both psychological and professional. Remember that Michael, the project manager described at the opening of this article, took a year off from project management to recover. But toxic handling can also take a physical toll. Most professional pain managers—be they counselors or psychiatrists—have been trained to recognize the physical warning signs of too much stress, such as stiff necks, nausea, and headaches. But toxic handlers are amateurs. Unlike workers at a real radioactive site, they do not have clothing, equipment, or procedures to protect them. They toil in danger zones completely exposed.

Dave Marsing is a case in point. In 1990, Marsing was assigned to turn around one of Intel's microprocessor fabrication plants near Albuquerque, New Mexico. The situation he inherited was dire: the plant's yield rates were bad and getting worse. The company's senior managers were pressing very hard for a quick solution to the problem. Employees were in pain, too, saying unrealistic pressure from above had them anxious and frustrated. "I was trying to be a human bridge between all the parts of the company and cope with all the emotions," Marsing recalls. "On the outside, I was soothing everybody, and work was getting back on track. But on the inside, I was in turmoil. I couldn't sleep, couldn't eat." Two months after Marsing arrived on the job, he suffered a near-fatal heart attack. He was 36 years old. (Currently the vice president of Intel's technology and manufacturing group and general manager of assembly and test manufacturing, Marsing says, "The heart attack was the result of a hereditary condition that got pushed over the edge from the stress.")

Savannah is another toxic handler who became physically ill after playing the role for several months. Like Rick in our earlier example, Savannah led a team assigned to implement a new program that based promotion on performance rather than seniority. Resistance was enormous, but in this case, the program went through. In the process, however, Savannah's team was brutalized by many members of the organization. "It was a case of 'kill the messenger,'" Savannah says. "All the anger and bitterness that people felt for top management were directed at us."

As a toxic handler, Savannah worked hard to protect her team from the worst of the attacks. A senior manager who opposed the new policy, for instance, sent a scathing and personally insulting letter to one team member. Savannah intercepted it and sent back a memo that instructed him to send all future correspondence directly to her. Another senior manager who was opposed to the policy tried to punish Savannah's team by moving it to smaller, less attractive office space. Savannah deflected the move, and her team stayed put, but, she recalls, "I was as stressed as I ever have been in my life. At work, I would be strong for my team, but at home,

I cried a lot. I slept away from my husband, although I didn't actually sleep very much, and often felt terribly depressed. The worst, though, were the panic attacks, which would come on so suddenly. My heart would pound, and I would lose my breath."

Dave Marsing and Savannah are not unusual. Many managers in our research told us of bouts of depression, severe heart palpitations, chronic sleeplessness, and cases of pneumonia.

These anecdotal cases are consistent with scientific evidence of a strong link between stress and illness. That link was first documented in the 1950s by Dr. Hans Selye, the renowned Canadian medical researcher who found that overwhelming stress leads to a breakdown of the protective mechanisms in the body—in other words, that stress compromises the body's immune system. In 1993, Bruce McEwen and Eliot Stellar reviewed two decades of research on the connection between stress and disease. Their analysis, published in the *Archives of Internal Medicine*, concluded that stress can compromise the immune system so severely that it raises blood pressure, weakens resistance to viral infections, increases the risk of heart attacks, and hastens the spread of cancer. Incidentally, the report says, stress puts intense pressure on the biological areas most susceptible to attack. Thus, if Harry's cardiovascular system is prone to weakness, his response to stress might be a heart attack. If Carmen's intestinal system is her weak spot, then stress for her may show up in chronic stomach ailments.

A study published in the *Journal of Advancement in Medicine* in 1995 demonstrated just how long the effects of stress can last. Researchers asked groups of healthy volunteers to focus on two emotions: either anger or compassion. Measures were then taken of a key immune

system antibody, secretory immunoglobulin A—called
IgA—which helps the body resist invading bacteria and
viruses.

The researchers found that when the volunteers spent
just five minutes remembering an experience that made
them feel angry or frustrated, their IgA levels increased
briefly then dropped substantially and stayed low for five
hours. When volunteers focused on feelings of care and
compassion, IgA levels rose and remained at a high level
for six hours. What this study suggests is that simply
remembering an emotion can have a strong impact on a
person's health. Consider the implications for toxic handlers. When they go home and remember the events of
their day, they certainly experience a drop in their IgA
levels that lasts for hours, since the act of remembering
surely lasts longer than five minutes at a time.

In addition to having an effect on the toxic handlers'
immune systems, the stress triggered by negative emotions can influence neural pathways in the brain. As people think repeatedly about what makes them angry,
stronger and stronger circuits are built in their brains.
That increases the level of emotional distress until a neural architecture is built that supports those feelings. They
become easier pathways to activate and run. They
become our hot buttons.

Thus, the situation for toxic handlers—who shoulder
the stress of others in addition to their own—would
seem to be all the more dangerous. "Caregivers are
human, too," says Dr. Michael Myers, a psychiatrist and
clinical professor at the University of British Columbia.
"As a specialist in physician health, I treat many physi-
cians each year for clinical depression. Those in administrative medicine tell me how hard it is to cope with the
problems of their staff doctors and other health profes-

sionals. The administrators have lost their ability to keep their armor in place."

Handling Toxic Handlers

The toll of managing organizational pain cannot be ignored: either organizations should better support toxic handlers in their role or they should make them unnecessary in the first place through practices that systematically manage and diffuse organizational pain. Our focus here will be on support because our years of experience studying organizational behavior, in addition to the prevalence of toxic handlers in our research, suggests that toxic handlers will be with us as long as organizations give rise to strong emotions. In other words, forever.

ACKNOWLEDGE THE DYNAMIC

The first step in supporting toxic handlers is for executives to acknowledge, simply, that toxic handlers exist and that they play a critical role. Of course, in reality, there is nothing simple about such a public admission. A culture of toughness infuses many organizations, and a high value is often placed on technical competence. Emotional competence is irrelevant; it doesn't show up on the bottom line, or so the thinking goes. And even if executives agree that someone has to manage pain, they still consider the job to be the corporate version of society's "women's work"—the stuff of daily life that must be done but is thankless. In most families, for instance, women answer the cries of babies in the night and care for elderly and infirm relatives. Women make Thanksgiving dinner, clean up afterward, and then smooth out the argument between a pair of uncles who drank too much.

People rarely acknowledge these efforts. Similarly, it would be quite a departure from business life as we know it for executives to show gratitude to those who practice emotional caretaking at work.

One other aspect of corporate life makes organizational pain a difficult, even dangerous, topic to bring to the table. Middle and senior managers are usually expected to tough it out during hard times. As one manager in our study recalls, "After a particularly bitter strike that churned up a lot of agony and anger, the company provided counseling for the workers. There was nothing for any managers. We were expected to suck in our emotions, stay quiet, and cope alone." Indeed, managers at the company felt, perhaps rightly, that to talk about their feelings would have hurt their careers.

Organizations must recognize the toxic handlers in their midst so that their important work can be supported before a crisis strikes.

And yet, despite the strong corporate ethic not to discuss organizational pain—let alone thank toxic handlers—we think that when executives do so, the effects are likely to be immediate and positive. Take the case of a team leader at a media company who had played the toxic-handling role during a brutal six-month merger process in which many employees lost their jobs. The team leader had managed to hit all of her financial goals during the upheaval, and she expected that would be the main focus of her performance review. It was. But if her boss had also focused on how the woman saved the emotional health of the merger's survivors, we are confident that her response would have been relief and pride, and perhaps renewed energy.

Raising consciousness about the toxic handler role requires that a forum be established in the company to talk about the topic. It needs, for instance, to get onto the agenda of management meetings or retreats, and it needs a champion to ensure that it gets sufficient time and attention in these settings. Of course, it is unrealistic to expect that toxic handling and its consequences will be discussed openly when its source is a toxic boss. The toxic boss needs to learn about the dynamic in a more neutral setting, such as a conference of senior managers from several organizations. (This could only happen in the best-case scenario, however, because toxic bosses often lack a high enough degree of self-awareness to apply the discussion to themselves.)

Organizations must realize that effective pain management can—and does—contribute to the bottom line.

Ultimately, a critical ingredient of any successful consciousness-raising about toxic handling is the recognition that effective pain management can—and does—contribute to the bottom line. No company can afford to let talented employees burn out. Nor can it afford to have a reputation as an unfriendly or unhappy place to work. Many good people simply won't join. It is essential, then, to make the business case for recognizing the work of toxic handlers. Otherwise, that role will stay in the closet, where most people are comfortable with it.

ARRANGE FOR TOXIC HANDLERS TO SHARE THEIR EXPERIENCES

Executives can minimize the toll on toxic handlers by bringing them together or by arranging for them to meet periodically with professionals who are trained to help them decompress and rejuvenate. Of course, this presumes that toxic handlers know who they are or can be readily identified. Thus the process of raising consciousness can be a very important precondition to setting up the necessary support for toxic handlers.

It is possible for handlers themselves to take the lead in making this happen. At one company we studied, toxic handlers spontaneously formed their own support group. The company was going through a period of rapid downsizing, and the burden of assuaging widespread sadness, fear, and anger fell largely to five managers. After a month of going it alone, the group members started to meet for dinner once a week to "let off steam," as one manager puts it. Another recalls, "One of the worst parts of the downsizing was that there was no quick bang of departures, just a slow, painful bleed. We were helping individuals to leave the organization on a nonstop basis. We were the ones who helped the managers prepare for the termination discussions and supported the employees when they received the news. Needless to say, it was a heavy emotional burden. The only way we got through it was to support one another. It was like a bereavement group, to tell you the truth— the thing that helped the most was just knowing I wasn't alone."

Executives shouldn't count on support groups forming on their own, however, especially since most toxic handlers pride themselves on a high tolerance for personal pain. As one CEO in our study notes, "These folks don't know when to ask for help; they're too busy giving it. And it would kill them to let others down by breaking down themselves." Better, then, to suggest that the organization's toxic handlers meet with one another, and even arrange such meetings. And better yet to bring in experts who can guide toxic handlers through conversations that allow them to see, understand, and appreciate the pressures of what they do. Experts can also help toxic handlers tell if they are dangerously close to burning out or presenting worrisome physical symptoms.

That's what happened to one manager in our study who had been a toxic handler for two years during a company restructuring. The manager tells us, "It took a therapist to help me to recognize that I was taking it into my gut. I was ignoring all the signs my body was sending me. I was taking things very personally. The therapist allowed me to hear myself in denial."

Finally, a professional can help some toxic handlers learn how to say no. One manager in our research tells us, "I learned that it was possible to say 'no' with options." Until that point, the manager had had a lot of trouble turning away people who needed to vent their emotions and, as a result, he was drowning under the workload of his real job and his toxic-handling role. "I learned that 'no' doesn't mean 'I don't care,' and it doesn't mean 'not ever.' It can mean, 'No, I can't do this, but I could do this.' Or, 'No, I can't help you now, but how about tomorrow?' Or, 'No, I can't help you, but let me find someone who can.'" That insight, the manager says, made work manageable again.

REASSIGN THE TOXIC HANDLER TO A SAFE ZONE

Even when other actions, such as counseling, can help toxic handlers deal with stress, it also makes sense to move them out of the stressful situation. These moves need not be long term. One company, for instance, sent a toxic handler who was showing signs of burnout to a two-week conference in Florida. The conference was work related—there were at least three hours of meetings a day—but also included heavy doses of rest and relaxation. It was, in essence, a bit of a forced vacation. There needs to be a high level of trust, openness, and cultural support in the organization for this solution to work. Otherwise, there is a distinct risk that toxic handlers will feel threatened by such an assignment and think they have done something wrong and that their career is in jeopardy.

Research conducted in 1995 confirms the healing power of taking breaks. André Delbecq of the Leavey School of Business at Santa Clara University and Frank Friedlander of the Fielding Institute in Santa Barbara, California, studied the habits and routines of 166 business leaders in the computer and health care industries who were known to be happy, healthy, and well balanced. All of the participants in the study worked in companies undergoing rapid change, and inasmuch, managed considerable organizational pain. The researchers found that while the leaders' habits and routines varied widely, they frequently took short (two- to five-day) vacations, typically with their families. "The breaks allowed the leaders to step back, regain a fresh perspective on themselves and their situations," Delbecq observed, "Each time, they returned to work like new people."

In extreme cases of organizational distress, however, a short break is not enough to restore a toxic handler, and organizations should consider reassigning them to parts of the company that are less in the throes of emotional distress. Naturally, most toxic handlers will resist. They value what they do and understand its importance to the organization's well-being. Thus, it is important that the

decision to relocate toxic handlers be thoroughly discussed with them. But when executives sense that a
manager is overloaded by the role, they must act despite
the toxic handler's objections. Later, when the spell is
broken, the toxic handlers may come to see the wisdom
of such an intervention and may even appreciate the
spirit in which it was done.

MODEL "HEALTHY" TOXIC HANDLING

If managing organizational pain is an open topic, then
managers can feel comfortable demonstrating how to do
it right. Following his heart attack, Dave Marsing made it
a point to show other managers how to stay calm at
work, even under intense pressure. "I try, to the greatest
extent possible, to maintain a level of calmness in the
face of frantic issues," he says. "I try to be as objective
as possible in discussions, and if I'm in a face-to-face
meeting with someone who

*Can an organization
systematically manage the
pain it generates—
making toxic handlers
unnecessary?*

has a short fuse, I'll sit right next to that person to make
sure the fuse is never lit. I do that by being calm, even
overly calm. When things get heated, I even change my
voice. I will consciously take a deeper breath, or two deep
breaths, in front of everybody to get them to calm down
a little bit and talk about the specifics, about solutions."

Marsing also encourages his staff to keep their work
and personal lives in balance. "When I coach the people
who report to me, who manage very large sites around
the company, I tell them how important it is to spend
more time with their families, to spend more time exercising, to get some help to assist them to work through

administrative things, rather than putting in extraordinarily long, tense days." Indeed, Marsing believes that teaching toxic handlers how to stay healthy in what is inherently an unhealthy role is one of his most important jobs as an executive.

MAKING TOXIC HANDLERS OBSOLETE

Can an organization systematically manage the emotional pain that it generates—making toxic handlers entirely unnecessary? It's unlikely, but our research has found several practices that remove from individuals the burden of alleviating emotional pain. Consider the practice of public grieving. In some organizations, executives create opportunities for employees to participate in rituals that, frankly, resemble funerals. For instance, when a Canadian company was acquired and folded into a former competitor from France, managers from the acquired business invited employees to a church-like ceremony where the company was eulogized by executives and hourly workers alike. Afterward, people went outside and, one by one, threw their old business cards into a coffin-shaped hole in the ground, which was then covered by dirt as a dirge played on a bagpipe. The event may sound ridiculous, but it did serve a healing purpose. Employees said later that they had buried their old company and were ready to embrace the new one.

The effectiveness of public grieving perhaps explains why Stanley Harris of Lawrence Technological University in Southfield, Michigan, and Robert Sutton of Stanford University's Department of Industrial Engineering, who studied dying organizations in the United States in the 1980s, were struck by "the prevalence of parties, picnics, and other social occasions during the final phases of organizational death. People had the opportunity to express sadness, anger, grief, perhaps in some cases even relief, during these ritualized ceremonies. Often people cried."

Another way companies can systematically manage organizational pain is to outsource the task. For instance, companies often hire consultants to steer or galvanize change initiatives. Some of these change experts are—by dint of experience—capable toxic handlers. If the toxic-handling role is explicitly given to them, then it won't as easily fall to in-house managers.

The following example from our research illustrates how outside consultants can effectively play the toxic-handling role during a change program. Two consultants from Deloitte Consulting worked closely with the client for three months. One of them, Heather McKay, remembers: "We got to know many of the company's key stakeholders, and in effect became the psychiatrists for the project. Because we provided an environment of anonymity, many people opened up with us to share their fears and reservations.

"I think our role as informal toxic handlers was helpful to employees in a couple of ways. We gave a number of individuals in the organization an outlet to release the pain they were carrying around with them rather than just transferring it amongst themselves. We also were in a position to stand back from the pain and help them to identify ways to reduce it. This is easier when you are not suffering from the pain yourself."

In the final analysis, then, bringing in external consultants to act as surrogate toxic handlers may make a great deal of sense. They can often be more objective than insiders, and they can also provide more pointed feed-back than managers who have to face their colleagues daily. One caveat, however: for external consultants to be effective toxic handlers, they must be trusted and credible. One Australian manager who attempted to hire external consultants to deal with a toxic situation in his company quickly found resistance because employees felt the outsiders didn't understand the painful situation well enough to help resolve it. "People in pain won't go to outsiders unless they believe the consultants really know how things are in the company," he says.

Finally, companies can systematically manage organizational pain by providing employees with stress training. Such training could decrease the demand for toxic handlers—people would be able to deal with their emotions on their own—and also help toxic handlers understand how to help themselves. Several stress-training programs exist. For example, one used by both Motorola and Hewlett-Packard during strategic change projects was developed by HeartMath in Boulder Creek, California. The program uses several techniques, such as Freeze-Frame, which teaches employees to recognize a stressful feeling, then freeze it—that is, take a time-out and breathe more slowly and deeply. Freeze-Frame concludes with steps based on the biomedical notion of improving balance in the autonomic nervous system, brain, and heart that help employees handle stress differently from their usual reflex reaction. Instead of impulsively jumping in to take over another person's pain, for example, employees are taught to catch their breath, collect their thoughts, connect with their emotions, and then ask the other person to analyze his or her own unhappiness. Returning a problem to its sender may seem like a minor change, but for toxic handlers, it is a radical departure from standard operating procedure.

Programs like those offered by HeartMath come at a price; they can run to $7,000 a day for up to 20 people. But they may well be worth the costs saved through greater retention and productivity.

In Good Company

When we began our research on managing emotional pain, we expected quite a bit of resistance—even denial—from senior executives. We did indeed find some of that. But much more often, we found executives who were aware that their organizations spawned anger, sadness, fear, and confusion as a matter of course. And we found scores of people who managed those feelings as toxic handlers themselves or watched with gratitude and concern as others did. In many cases, our interviews about toxic handling were highly charged. Some cried as they recalled its demands; others felt anger. A few spoke of remorse.

Mainly, our research unearthed feelings of relief. Executives and middle managers alike indicated that this was the first time they had been able to talk about organizational pain. We are sure that it is neither possible, nor even desirable, to remove all pain in organizations. Emotional pain comes not only from downsizing, bad bosses, and change. It also accompanies the commitment and passion of individuals striving for excellence. Nevertheless, managing the pain of others, whatever its source, is hard work. It needs to be given the attention and support it deserves for everyone's benefit—the health of employees is a key element in the long-term competitiveness of companies and of our society. People who have felt alone in managing organizational pain, or in caring for people who do, should know that they are in good company.

More Than a Job

THE SEEMINGLY THANKLESS TASK of fronting for a toxic boss begs the question, Why do toxic handlers do it? That is, why do some people take on the emotional pain of their organizations? After all, few are openly rewarded for it. As a former senior vice president in the banking industry who was a toxic handler tells us, "You have to get your reward for doing this kind of work within yourself because you rarely get recognition from the corporation."

In some cases, toxic handlers emerge as a result of their position in the organization, usually as a manager in the human resources department. But more often, toxic handlers are pulled into the role—bit by bit—by their colleagues, who turn to them because they are trustworthy, calm, kind, and nonjudgmental.

Of course, it is possible to say "I'm sorry, I don't have the time" to needy coworkers. But the people who become toxic handlers are predisposed to say yes. Many have done so their entire lives—playing toxic handler at home and in school. These individuals often have a high tolerance for pain themselves, plus a surplus of empathy. Moreover, they read every situation for its emotionality—that is, they quickly notice when people are in pain and feel compelled to make the situation right. Indeed, if some toxic handlers had not gone into business, they would probably have become counselors or therapists.

A skeptic might suppose that toxic handlers must be emotionally unbalanced themselves, suffering from the "savior complex" that afflicts some social workers or from an unhealthy desire to be needed. Some might accuse them of being bleeding hearts, who feel sorry for everyone they meet. And still others might see in toxic handlers—in particular, those who work with toxic bosses—a tendency toward enabling or codependent behavior. As anyone who has studied alcoholism or drug addiction knows, both types of relationships are very unhealthy.

But in our research, we did not encounter toxic handlers of the ilk described above. Instead, we found professional managers who happened to be highly attuned to the human aspects of their organizations. And as one manager who has observed toxic handlers in his organization notes: "These people are usually relentless in their drive to accomplish organizational targets and rarely lose focus on business issues. Managing emotional pain is one of their means." We would suggest it is also a calling.

Originally published in July–August 1999
Reprint 99406

Leadership in a Combat Zone

WILLIAM G. PAGONIS

Executive Summary

LIEUTENANT GENERAL WILLIAM G. PAGONIS led the 40,000 men and women who ran the theater logistics in the Persian Gulf War during its three phases of operation: Desert Shield (buildup), Desert Storm (ground war), and Desert Farewell (redeployment). By military standards, it was a challenging assignment. By the conventions of any nonmilitary complex organization, it was unheard of.

In the Persian Gulf, Pagonis's challenges included feeding, clothing, sheltering, and arming over 550,000 people. All of this in a hostile desert region with a Muslim community distrustful of the "infidels" sent there to protect them. The lessons of leadership gleaned through Pagonis's experiences in the Gulf cross military boundaries—they apply equally to general management and leadership development in the private, civilian sector.

113

To gain a clear sense of the overall organization in an area the size of the Southwest Asian theater, Pagonis deputized proxies, dubbed "Ghostbusters," to be his eyes and ears throughout the desert. His goal was to build a leadership-supporting environment, combining centralized control with decentralized execution. Pagonis believes vision is defined by the leader, but subordinates define the objectives that move the organization toward the desired outcome. The roots of leadership, Pagonis claims, are expertise and empathy. A leader's work is not only to apply these traits but also to cultivate them—both on a personal and organizational level. True leaders create organizations that themselves cultivate leadership. This can only be achieved through rigorous and systematic organizational development.

Lieutenant General William G. Pagonis led the 40,000 men and women who ran the theater logistics for the Persian Gulf War during its three phases of operation: Desert Shield (buildup), Desert Storm (ground war), and Desert Farewell (redeployment). By military standards, it was a challenging assignment. By the conventions of any non-military, complex organization, it was unheard of. Over the course of a few hectic months, his organization, the 22nd Support Command, grew from 5 people to 40,000. The team fed, clothed, sheltered, and armed over 550,000 people. They served 122 million meals. Within the theater, they transported and distributed more than 7 million tons of supplies, 117,000 wheeled vehicles, 2,200 tracked vehicles, and 2,000 helicopters. They pumped 1.3 billion gallons of fuel. They successfully supported General

Norman Schwarzkopf's "end run" strategy, and did so in a harsh environment with almost no preexisting military infrastructure.

The 22nd Support Command's accomplishments are testimony to an often maligned branch of the Army. Logistics, at best, has been traditionally dismissed as mundane. But the lessons of leadership gleaned through Pagonis's experience in the Gulf cross military boundaries—they apply equally to general management and leadership development in the private, civilian sector.

Lt. General Pagonis is author (with Jeffrey L. Cruikshank) of Moving Mountains: Lessons in Leadership and Logistics from the Gulf War *(Harvard Business School Press, 1992).*

IT HAS BEEN A YEAR and a half since I completed my tour of duty in Saudi Arabia as head of the United States Army's 22nd Support Command. And in the wake of the Allied victory over Iraq, I've read and thought a lot about my logistics profession. But I've also done a great deal of thinking about the goals, qualities, and prerequisites of leadership. And based on that reflection, I've reached a number of conclusions.

For one, I've concluded that leadership is only possible where the ground has been prepared in advance. To a certain extent, I'll be the first to admit, this process of ground-breaking is beyond the control of a lone individual in a large organization. If the organization isn't pulling for you, you're likely to be hobbled from the start. Fortunately for me and for thousands of other officers like me, the Army goes to great lengths—greater, I would argue, than any other organization—to groom and develop its leaders. Like my peers in the general officer ranks, I have been formally educated, informally mentored, and systematically rotated through a wide variety of postings, all designed to challenge me in appropriate ways (that is, to push me without setting me up to fail) and to broaden my skills and knowledge base.

But a leader is not simply a passive vessel into which the organization pours its best intentions. To lead successfully, a person must demonstrate two active, essential, and interrelated traits: expertise and empathy. In my experience, both of these traits can be deliberately and systematically cultivated; this personal development is the first important building block of leadership.

A true leader must demonstrate two active, essential, and interrelated traits: expertise and empathy.

The leadership equation has another vital piece as well. Leaders are not only shaped by the environment; they also take active roles in remaking that environment in productive ways. In other words, true leaders create organizations that support the exercise and cultivation of leadership. This can only be achieved through rigorous and systematic organizational development.

The work of leadership, therefore, is both personal and organizational. The bad news is that this means hard work—lots of it. The good news is that leaders are made, not born. I'm convinced that anyone who wants to work hard enough and develop these traits can lead.

Charisma, Presence, and Other Notions

No military commander would downplay the importance of personal presence in leadership. It's a vital attribute, particularly in a combat setting. Almost every combat-hardened officer can recall that fateful moment of truth when his or her command presence was first put to the test.

In my own case, that test came in 1968, during my first tour in Vietnam. My boat company had already more than proven its mettle, transporting artillery barges and supplies through intermittent sniper fire up and down the rivers of the Mekong Delta. But during the Tet Offensive of February, we were beset and besieged as never before.

Late one night, we received word that an orphanage was under attack and that we needed to transport troops to the site as quickly as possible. Leaving our artillery barges behind, we took about 30 volunteers in 6 boats and went 5 miles downriver. I wasn't told at the time, but the rest of my outfit was then ordered to follow along behind with our artillery barges in tow.

My small convoy had just landed the infantry troops near the orphanage when I got a radio call that our trailing barges were stopped dead in the water. The first barge had come under fire and "crabbed"—gone sideways in the river—and now two dozen boats were trapped behind the barge. Our battalion commander got on the air, advised us of the extreme danger upriver, and ordered us not to go back and rescue our comrades.

It was a moonlit night. From where we sat, chafing under our orders to stay put, we could look upriver and see the tracers burning across the water where the boats were stuck. They were in deep trouble. On the spur of the moment, following a time-honored military tradition, I developed "radio trouble"—that is, I turned the communications gear off—and addressed the crew of four on my small patrol boat. "We've got to go back and help," I told them, "but I don't want to force you. Anyone who doesn't want to join can stay here, no questions asked."

I'm proud to say that every one of those soldiers volunteered. We turned one of our boats around and headed upriver with tracers zinging over our heads and bullets bouncing off the sides of the boat. When we reached the crabbed barge, I could see that the man behind the steering wheel had frozen. I jumped from my boat onto the barge, and shook him back into action. In short order, we got the boat turned around and headed home again.

One leader's orders had been ignored, and another's followed. Why? Adrenaline was one contributing factor. So was loyalty: our comrades needed help immediately. But most important was my soldiers' trust in my judgment. Had I not already earned that trust and developed a command presence in a thousand undramatic settings, those soldiers would not have followed my lead. Had I not demonstrated my confidence that we could pull off the rescue, they would not have followed. My troops would have taken the sensible course and followed the radio's lead.

This same lesson applies to leaders in private industry. We are misled by the popular-culture portrayals of leaders. Movies and television have to deal in superficialities and sound bites. They have to emphasize charisma—a mysterious and seductive quality. But when they do so, they overlook the real roots of leadership.

Expertise and Empathy

I can think of no leader, military or business, who has achieved his or her position without some profound expertise. Most leaders first achieve mastery in a particular functional area, such as logistics, and eventually move into the generalist's realm.

Expertise grows out of hard work and, to some extent, luck. It's hard work that develops a skill base, and it's often luck that gives us the chance to apply that base. Throughout my childhood, my parents ran small businesses: first a restaurant, and then a small hotel with a restaurant. Every member of the family was expected to pitch in. For my part, I scrubbed floors, waited on tables, did kitchen-prep, and helped keep the books. All through high school and college, my responsibilities expanded. I learned new things and kept my hand in old things.

After college graduation and ROTC training, I sought and won an Army commission. My first assignment was at Fort Knox, where those years of hands-on business training proved immediately useful in streamlining the unit's mail operations. On the strength of this success, I was asked to tackle the mess hall. This was even easier: I was already a minor expert in private-sector mess halls. Because I had expertise, I was successful; and because I was successful, I was identified by my superiors as a potential leader.

There are dozens of instances where I've grumbled my way through an assignment only to discover that the assignment has taught me a great deal, and that this learning is applicable in unexpected ways. Back in 1971, for example, I suffered through a stint of desk-bound research in which I was part of a team charged with analyzing LOTS (logistics-over-the-shore) vehicles. I was sure I was wasting my time, crunching numbers and drafting memos rather than leading troops.

Exactly 20 years later, I was in charge of—among several other resources—a flotilla of LOTS ships, which plied the coasts of Saudi Arabia serving as a backup for our truck convoys. Because I had been a member of the team that helped specify their design, I knew exactly how to use those vessels. I had expertise, which not only helped me do my job but also reinforced me as a leader in the eyes of my subordinates.

Owning the facts is a prerequisite to leadership. But there are millions of technocrats out there with lots of facts in their quiver and little leadership potential. In many cases, what they are missing is empathy. No one is a leader who can't put himself or herself in the other person's shoes. Empathy and expertise command respect.

I got my first inkling of this back in the 1950s, when I was a newsboy in my hometown of Charleroi, Pennsylvania. I started out at the age of nine, hawking afternoon editions of the *Charleroi Mail* on the corner of 5th and McKean. Things started going along pretty well for me there. I had regular customers, and I could shout out the headlines with the best of them: "Korean armistice signed! Read all about it!"

I soon began to notice, though, that the real market for papers was in the local bars and restaurants, rather than on quiet street corners like my own. At my little stand, I was averaging 50 copies a day. In the bars and restaurants, especially around dinner time, you could sell that many copies in two hours—and get tips, to boot.

Brash I was, even foolhardy. So I took a few licks, but I wouldn't back down.

I decided to mine this rich vein of opportunity. But the older newsboys, mostly 14 and 15 years old, dominated the commercial district, and they didn't appreciate my efforts to compete. A group of them paid me a visit, gave me a few licks, and suggested that I stick to my quiet little corner and stay out of their restaurants.

I did just that—for a little while. Then I went right back to selling papers in those crowded barrooms. Brash I was, even foolhardy; but I wasn't dumb. The opportunity was very good. And even then, I had a keen sense of justice. Why should the big kids control the best territory just because that was the way it had always been done? Even to the nine-year-old Gus Pagonis it was obvious that if you were going to do business, you'd better do it in the right place, and the big boys controlled the right place. I took a few more licks, but soon established myself as a savvy young businessman who wouldn't back down from a fight. I gained the older boys' respect and they no longer bothered me.

Years went by, and I gradually moved up in the newsboy hierarchy. Then one day I had a disturbing realization. I was now the "establishment." I was one of those big boys whom the young up-and-comers had to go up against. It seemed that I had a clear choice. I could perpetuate the cycle, or I could act in the spirit of empathy, based on my vivid recollection of what it felt like to get knocked around. I chose the latter course. At my urging, we came up with an arrangement that didn't cut too deeply into the profits of the veteran newsboys yet still gave the younger kids a chance to flex their entrepreneurial muscles. My peers went along with the plan because they knew I understood the situation from all sides. And I had earned a leader's respect from the younger kids through empathy.

Empathy was an absolutely vital quality in the context of the Gulf War. We asked ourselves constantly: What do the other people on our team need? Why do they think they need it, and how can we give it to them? The military always has its share of bendable rules. Can we find one to fit each situation?

Our hosts, the Saudi Arabian people and their government, were among the most important objects of this kind of attention. King Fahd had pledged his country's complete support and cooperation, and the Saudis delivered on that promise unstintingly. But both sides knew that the deployment of a half-million "infidels" into a strict Muslim society would be a daunting challenge.

We made our share of mistakes. Early in the most hectic phase of the Desert Shield deployment, for example, we decided to establish an Allied medical materiel command in the port city of Ad Dammam. American soldiers, male and female, reported to the site to unload boxes and crates of supplies. Unfortunately, we had no idea that the building we were moving into was located next to a particularly devout Muslim community, whose members were deeply offended by the sight of women with uncovered hair and rolled-up sleeves, working up a good sweat in the desert sun. Members of the community complained to the local religious police, and our female soldiers were soon subjected to catcalls and jeering.

Before the situation developed into a crisis, U.S. military leaders met with the appropriate Saudi religious and civil officials to get a handle on the cause of the disturbances. We soon reached a simple compromise: all U.S. military personnel would henceforth wear long-sleeved shirts in the city, and our female soldiers would keep their hair covered with their hats. It was a small concession, but one that greatly pleased the religious police responsible for enforcing the Sharia, or Islamic law.

We learned a great deal about the sensitivities of a Muslim community through these negotiations, and we applied the lessons in our subsequent dealings with the

Saudi population. We also took our learning one step further. It was clear that our hosts were inclined to avoid conflict with their 550,000 guests, at least until things were approaching a crisis stage. It was our responsibility, therefore, to anticipate their needs and avoid crises. One day several months after the ground war ended, I realized that our two inactivated firing ranges were still littered with unexploded ordnance, and that the bedouins would soon be traversing these areas again. We put ourselves in the shoes of the bedouins and also in the shoes of the Saudi officials who had to protect the interests of these desert wanderers. We cleaned up the ranges well before the Saudi Arabians had to put pressure on us to do so. With that we earned their continued respect and cooperation.

Empathy also helps you know where you can draw the line and make it stick. For example, some Saudi Arabians disapproved of the U.S. female soldiers driving vehicles and carrying weapons (activities in which Saudi Arabian women do not engage). I made it clear that from the U.S. Army's perspective, a soldier was a soldier, and that our lean logistical structure absolutely demanded that all our soldiers be allowed to use the tools of their trade. That line stuck.

Terrorist attacks were still a possibility, and the tragedy in Beirut was fresh in our minds.

Empathy counts for even more on the individual level. This was brought home to me one afternoon in August 1991, some six months into Desert Farewell. A very young private was sent to me by the military police for disciplinary action. The facts of the incident were clear enough. On the previous night, two MPs had demanded to see the private's ID. He cussed them out and wound up spending the night in jail. He arrived in my office looking remorseful and more than a little bit scared, and launched into a hurried and jumbled explanation. It was hot the night before, he said; he was tired, the MPs were picking on him, and so on. But when he finished making his excuses, he said simply, "I screwed up. I shouldn't have done it."

I made him think things through from the MPs' point of view. They had a job to do. Terrorist attacks were still a very real possibility, and the recent tragedies in Beirut and Berlin were very much in our minds. Tight security and ID checks were therefore still needed to protect the safety of everyone at the base. Then, after telling my wayward private that I would personally thank the MPs for their vigilance, I let him off the hook. He was out of my office in a flash.

Why did I bend the rules? Because empathy demanded it. This was a tough period. The war was long since over, and the vast majority of Coalition forces were already back in their home countries. But we logisticians were still there, picking up and packing up the theater. We were fighting a subtle battle against the perception that the "important" work of the war had already been accomplished, that the danger was past, that we were only mopping up after the main event. And, in fact, the weather *was* very hot—hotter than earlier in the summer when smoke from the oil fires in Kuwait had blocked out the sun. Inevitably, some tempers were wearing thin in the ranks. My young private had already learned his lesson, and he was more useful to me outside the brig than in.

The Steps of Leadership

I had the very good fortune early in my Army career to serve as an aide to a general officer in Germany. In that context, I visited most of the battalions and companies around the country. This was the military equivalent of a control experiment, in the sense that all of the commanders in the division were working on the same mission. But each of them approached his assignment a little bit differently—how he took care of his troops, how he briefed the results of his actions, how he presented himself. From company to company, and from battalion to battalion, what was really changing was leadership.

Even from my youthful and uninformed vantage point, it was obvious that some things worked and others didn't. And over time, I was able to distill the techniques of effective leadership that would work best for me. Cultivating leadership in yourself and in others should be done on both a personal and organizational level.

The first important step in the process of developing effective leadership may seem self-evident: *know yourself.* What's your expertise? What are your strengths? And, just as important, what are your weaknesses and how can you improve? Regularly scheduled self-examinations are a must for building and sustaining leadership.

Once you've assessed the raw material, you can draw up a plan that builds on your existing skills and knowledge. Take any steps necessary to sharpen those talents you already have or to compensate for ones you lack. Most leaders engage in public speaking, for example. Are you one of those rare leaders who can get away without making public appearances? Or could you benefit from some coaching in voice projection and deportment?

This kind of self-analysis allows you to be *real*—in my experience, a vital contributing factor in effective leadership. A person who is always playing to his or her weaknesses can't inspire much confidence in others. This is something to watch out for in matters large and small, since it's the cornerstone of presence. For example, I use a gentle kind of humor quite a bit. Humor helps me make contact with other people. But I only use humor because it comes naturally to me. I'm real when I use it. Those who aren't, shouldn't! In the same spirit, truly hopeless public speakers—of whom there are very few, by the way—should concentrate on grooming effective proxies.

A related challenge is to *learn how and what to communicate.* This comprises not only good speaking skills but also good listening skills and the ability to project and interpret body language. Many years ago, I set up formal systems to elicit constructive criticism from my subordinates. One of the first criticisms I got back was that I didn't listen well. This surprised me. Up to that moment, I thought my listening skills were as good as the next person's—maybe better. I poked around, asked questions, and eventually discovered that one basis for this judgment was a bad habit on my part. While listening to others, I had a tendency to sift quickly through mail or do an initial sort of my paperwork. My body language projected a lack of attention. With minor adjustments to my routine (maintaining eye contact during these meetings, relegating paperwork to later in the day), my report card improved. I also took to heart the advice of a wise commanding officer who said: "Never pass up the opportunity to remain silent." My subordinates soon began citing my listening skills as a strength rather than a weakness.

A third vital aspect of personal development relates directly to expertise: the leader has to *know the mission.* What needs to be accomplished? How can your expertise most effectively be channeled to do the job? This is an important part of the hard work I mentioned earlier. Leaders have to do their homework!

During the Gulf War, I directed my planning team to compile a binder, known within the command as the "Red Book," which was a complete and constantly updated collection of data outlining the developments of the conflict. Some four inches thick with charts and tables, it contained virtually all of the information I needed to keep abreast of our situation. While I was in transit from one theater location to another, that book was practically joined to me at the hip. General Schwarzkopf (or another general in the field or stateside) would frequently call me on the road or in the air with requests for specific information: how many tanks here, how much fuel there, how quickly can equipment be moved somewhere, and so on. I know that both my subordinates and superiors were regularly impressed with my almost magical grasp of the numbers. No magic was involved, I just studied that binder every chance I could.

When the elements of personal leadership development are in place, a leader can concentrate on building an appropriate context for leadership. Not surprisingly, this kind of organizational development depends, in large part, on a leader's ability to empower and motivate others to lead.

Moving Outward: Organizational Development

By definition, leaders don't operate in isolation. Nor do they command in the literal sense of the word, issuing a one-way stream of unilateral directives. Instead, leadership almost always involves cooperation and collaboration, activities that can occur only in a conducive context.

I am convinced that an effective leader can create such a context. My goal, as I set out to build a leadership-supporting environment, is to combine centralized control with decentralized execution.

This involves, first, extensive delegation. In a sense, this prerequisite is a logical extension of the personal awareness and development described above. A person who knows his or her expertise and the mission can find the right people to fill gaps. As a result, authority is pushed further and further down into the organization.

Delegation is only half of the story, though. The other piece involves system-building to ensure that the right information flows back up through the organization to the leader. This is a special challenge in an organization as traditionally bureaucratic as the Army. ("Staff grows, paper flows, no one knows," as the old saying has it.) But I suspect it's true for all human organizations.

Organizational development, then, includes a delicate balance of effective delegation and system-building. Over the years, I have developed a number of techniques and tools that help maintain this balance and ensure a smooth-running operation.

The first of these techniques is to *shape the vision.* Simple is better, since delegation depends on a shared understanding of the organizational goal. In the Gulf, we coined short sentences that captured the aim of our organization. These little nuggets were then aggressively disseminated. During the deployment phase, for example, you couldn't walk 20 feet within our headquarters without encountering the message, "Good logistics is combat power!" During the redeployment phase, safety was the overriding priority, and the vision became, "Not one more life!" Napkins, banners, buttons, newsletters: every possible tool was used toward building and underscoring a shared vision.

Vision must be defined by the leader. But it is the subordinates who must *define the objectives* that move the organization toward the desired outcome. "Objectives," in my lingo, are the concrete steps by which the vision will be realized. They must be specific and quantifiable. They should give subordinates the opportunity both to act and to assess the impact of their actions. For example: in my terminology, "win one for the Gipper" is a statement of vision. By contrast, "average 3.5 yards per carry on runs off tackle" is an objective articulated to advance the vision.

It's better to think through the Sunday game on Saturday than to kick the corpse on Monday.

A second key responsibility of the leader in building a leadership-supporting organization is to *educate*. On the first day a new person enters my command, I hold an orientation session to clarify my personal style, the organization of the command, our vision, and our shared objectives. Everyone needs to start off with the same information base. I specifically direct new arrivals to read my notebook of bulletins—a series of memoranda in which I have codified the key methods and tools of my command. The bulletins remain in a central location where they can be accessed by any member of the command at any time.

In addition, I regularly hold educational meetings, informally referred to as "skull sessions." These involve gathering a large group of people from many functional areas into one room and leading them through a discussion of how they would handle a range of hypothetical-but-plausible challenges. The goal, I tell them at the outset of the meeting, is to "do our Monday-morning quarterbacking on Saturday night." (In other words, better to think through the Sunday game in advance than to kick the corpse on Monday.) Through this device, my people are challenged to think in collaborative ways, to be aware of the real complexity of most situations, to become comfortable asking each other for advice and help, and, most important, to anticipate problems.

For the benefit of both the individual and the larger organization, it is vital to *give and get feedback*. Of course, every interaction with a subordinate, peer, or superior is an opportunity to do just that and should be used accordingly. But I've also found the need to implement a number of mechanisms to reinforce the feedback loop.

The organizational effectiveness (OE) session is one such tool. Once or twice a year, I take my top-level officers out of their normal routines for a one- or two-day organizational "retreat." On neutral ground, we go through role-playing exercises, take time for relaxation, and do some formal feedback exercises.

In this context, I've hit on one small innovation that helps to keep things productive. Each member of the command is asked to evaluate the person to his or her left. In doing so, the evaluator must identify three positive qualities in the person being scrutinized, as well as three areas where that person could improve his or her performance. Criticism tends to be taken more easily when it is not perceived as an attack. It was in this context, in fact, that I first learned about my bad listening skills—and, as we all know, the higher the rank, the harder to teach.

My second favored method for giving feedback has been a formal part of the Army organization for quite some time: the Evaluation Report. I put a personal twist on the ER by making it a multistep process. The conventional ER is a one-step process. After a subordinate has been in a given position for about a year, the superior officer fills out a written form rating the subordinate's performance. The problem is that the subordinate can perform below standard and never know it until a damning evaluation is filed away in the personnel files. This shortchanges everybody—the individual, the evaluator, and certainly the organization.

In my command, the ER is a two- or even three-step process. Each individual is evaluated about one or two months into his or her tenure in a position. During this meeting, the superior points out areas of the job at which the ratee is particularly accomplished and identifies other areas that need work. In the months that follow, each individual has an opportunity to develop and improve his or her skills before the final evaluation report. In the meantime, the organization benefits from improved productivity and open communication.

In complex organizations, it is important to *emphasize formal communication* with structures designed to complement the chain of command. My notebook of bulletins is one such tool. There are many others.

My work days, for example, are punctuated by a series of meetings. The first is the daily "stand-up," attended by at least one representative of each functional area in the command. (During the Gulf War, the stand-up was a chance for people to make quick status reports and then field questions.) At the end of each day, we hold a "sit-down" meeting, which gives us a chance to engage in a more concentrated kind of analysis. The sit-down also uses a "three-up, three-down" device similar to the one employed in my OE sessions. Each functional commander reports daily on three areas in his or her command that are improving and three areas that need attention.

In between these two meetings are other communications devices. For example, a few hours of my afternoon are divided into 15-minute segments called "Please See Me" time. When someone's ideas have puzzled or intrigued me, I ask them to come in and talk during one of these slots. In addition, any member of the command who has a question or a problem can sign up for a quarter-hour slot.

For straight talk, nothing compares with what I hear during my daily basketball game with the troops.

This part of the scheduling process is completely democratic. Any member of the command can sign up for a meeting, and no one ever gets bounced through rank-pulling.

And finally, there's my favorite low-tech, high-yield information transfer system: the 3 inch by 5 inch index card. I stumbled upon the 3 x 5 as a mode of communication completely by accident early in my career, and I've used it ever since. In the Gulf, questions or comments written on a 3 x 5 were guaranteed to move through the chain of command (informing appropriate personnel along the way) until they reached someone with the knowledge and authority to respond to them, and then they were returned to their authors—all within 24 hours, guaranteed. During the height of the conflict, I got about 100 a day, and every one was useful.

Formal methods of information transfer are very important, but I find that you don't get a complete view of what's actually happening in an organization unless you also open regular informal communication channels. For straight talk, nothing compares with the comments I pick up during my daily basketball game with the troops. Similarly, when my wife and I invite troops into our home for a lasagna dinner, we hope to show them that we, too, are human and approachable.

Sometimes the soldiers come to me; other times, I go to them. I devote a good deal of my time to "management by walking around." In the Gulf, MBWA took me from the frontline logbases where ammunition, food, and fuel were distributed to the troops, to the materiel dumps. I spent time with the MPs guarding the main supply routes and the "washrack" jocks responsible for cleaning and sterilizing the tanks and helicopters we were about to send home. I visited enemy prisoner-of-war camps that had been hastily erected as the ground war ended, the docks and airfields, and a hundred other more or less remote facilities.

I worked hard to be a real and constant presence throughout the desert, in all parts of the command. But the Southwest Asian theater was so large that I couldn't be in enough places often enough. Recognizing that fact, I deputized a group of soldiers—dubbed the "Ghostbusters"—as my proxies. They went into the desert as my official eyes and ears, making sure everything was running smoothly, giving and gaining a clearer sense of the theater's overall organization.

That was the point of all of this meeting, mentoring, and moving around? In a sense, it was to touch as many people, and as many kinds of people, as possible. Leaders must be motivators, educators, role models, sounding boards, confessors, and cheerleaders—they must be accessible, and they must aggressively pursue contact with colleagues and subordinates.

Muscle Memory: A Concluding Thought

Successful leadership is not mysterious. Leaders must set their own agendas and use the tools and techniques best suited to help them achieve their goals. But leadership is not entirely formulaic. Leaders must learn to trust their instincts and play their hunches.

When the fighting ended in the Gulf, an Army unit was asked to make the physical preparations for the peace talks. As the talks grew near, I developed a strange conviction—a gnawing in the pit of my stomach—that something wasn't right up in Safwan, Iraq, site of the talks. The night before the meetings were scheduled to start, I commandeered a Black Hawk helicopter to go up and take a look and discovered that the job was less than half completed. The necessary supplies had been caught in a monumental traffic jam and hadn't gotten through. Through a superhuman effort, working all night with the materials that were at hand, we made it possible for the peace talks to proceed on schedule. (I'm sure that history will record only that General Pagonis inexplicably fell asleep during the talks and slipped off his chair!)

It is said that once a basketball player practices his shots enough times, he develops a "muscle memory" of how to sink those shots. Only then is he truly free to improvise on the court. Similarly, I'm convinced that if someone works hard at leadership, his or her instincts will tend to be right. His or her hunches will be based on expertise and empathy, and they'll be good ones. Leadership will seem to come easily.

Originally published in November–December 1992
Reprint 92607

September 11, 2001

A CEO's Story

JEFFREY W. GREENBERG

Executive Summary

ON THE DAY OF THE TERRORIST ATTACKS on New York's World Trade Center, 1,779 employees of Marsh & McLennan Companies had office space in the twin towers, and another 129 were visiting that day. From his office at MMC headquarters in midtown, CEO Jeffrey Greenberg watched in horror as the second plane hit. By the time the towers fell, he had gathered a team of his colleagues to begin to outline how the company would respond.

In this first-person account, Greenberg relates what it was like to manage through the unimaginable. The needs of MMC's people, and the families of employees who perished, took top priority. In the midst of chaos and unforeseeable problems, Greenberg and his colleagues improvised ways of communicating and assembled a broad-based program of support. Help appeared from all sides, from people of various ranks, titles, and functional expertise within MMC as well as past chairmen, outside directors, and retired executives.

An emergency communications center was immediately set up at MMC headquarters and became a centralized location for messages and information and a memorial to colleagues lost in the attacks. The company arranged for grief counselors and established a family assistance center and a Family Relationship Management Program for those who had lost MMC employees. It has also provided families with access to long-term psychological and financial counseling.

At the same time, Greenberg offers lessons about leadership, company culture, and adaptability. He and his colleagues held responsibility for a business beset by operational destruction and financial losses and facing dramatically changed market conditions. Their resolve was not simply to keep it on course but to come back stronger than ever.

ON SEPTEMBER 11, 2001, Marsh & McLennan Companies had 1,908 people working in or visiting our offices in the twin towers of the World Trade Center. Eight hundred forty-five worked on floors 93 to 100 of One World Trade Center—the floors directly in the path of the first hijacked airliner to hit the buildings. Nine hundred thirty-four worked in the second tower, on floors 48 through 54. One hundred twenty-nine visiting from other offices had meetings scheduled in the buildings. We also had an employee who was a passenger on one of the planes. These are facts I can tell you with certainty; we have lived with them day and night ever since. What I cannot do is convey the grief we felt that day and the loss that stays with us.

As I write this, we are approaching the first anniversary of September 11. We have assisted the families of lost colleagues, relocated employees, recaptured data, and restored business capabilities. We can never completely recover from our human losses. We will always live with the consequences of September 11. But enough time has passed to reflect on the impact of the terrorist attacks on the company and our response to them—how we have mourned our losses, supported the families and one another, and continued to serve our clients.

The Day the World Changed

I had just arrived at my office that morning when a colleague grabbed me and told me to come to the south windows. MMC's headquarters in midtown Manhattan has an unobstructed view to the tip of lower Manhattan. Everyone else on the floor was already at those windows, looking with horror at smoke rising from a gash in One World Trade Center. As we struggled to make sense of what had happened—Had a small plane hit it? How could that happen on such a clear morning?—we saw a fireball erupt from the second tower. Suddenly we realized that the Trade Center—perhaps the country—was under attack.

I think I was the only person who left the windows. Everyone else was glued to the scene, trying to phone colleagues in the two buildings. I needed to get to my office and start dealing with what this atrocity meant for MMC. Were people getting out of the buildings? Had we lost people? Which facilities were affected? Which clients were affected? What could we do? Where should we start? My phone was out. I had a TV moved in to get news; it remained on for the next week. By ten o'clock, I had gathered a group of managers in a nearby conference room, and we were beginning to figure out what needed to be done.

Veterans of combat talk about the "fog of war" that prevails in conflict; we were facing that same kind of fog. Our communication lines were down, and news from the outside world was confused and contradictory. We had sketchy information that employees of Guy Carpenter, our reinsurance subsidiary headquartered in Tower Two, were evacuating, but we didn't know who was safe and who wasn't and whether there would be more attacks. Suddenly, any possible mechanism for getting information had to be considered, and nothing we would normally rely upon was reliable. Meanwhile, our midtown building was filled with people who were shocked, frightened, and desperate for guidance.

With the hope of helping our employees cope with the situation, I got on the emergency public-address system later that morning. Until then, I couldn't have told you that we had a PA system in our building. But I soon got to know it well. That first message conveyed everything we knew and no speculation beyond that: "As you know, both towers of the World Trade Center have been hit by airplanes. We have employees in both towers." I went on to inform people that colleagues on the 48th floor of the second tower had been evacuated and that transportation out of Manhattan had been shut down. I promised an update as soon as more information became available.

The group I had pulled together to organize our immediate response was mixed in rank, title, and functional expertise. As would have been the case on any given day, some of our senior people were out of town;

the moratorium on air travel meant that some of them wouldn't be back for days. We worked with those who were here, using our existing disaster-recovery and business-continuity plans when possible and improvising when necessary. Very quickly, we outlined four major areas of concern and assigned people to head task forces on each of them. The first, of course, focused on our people. We had to find out where everyone was and determine what sort of help we could provide. The second was communications. We knew that as soon as our phones and e-mail system came back, we'd be flooded with calls and inquiries. Moreover, many people would need to hear from us. Third, there were numerous operational issues. We needed to be able to serve clients, some of whom would no doubt be severely affected by the attacks. Our World Trade Center facilities had included the headquarters of one division, a data center housing servers for another, and telecommunications equipment. And the fourth concern was the financial effect on our ability to do business.

Our people and their needs were far and away the top priority. Immediately, we made the decision to convert part of the 35th floor of our headquarters, which holds meeting rooms and the company cafeteria, into an emergency communications center. We ran wires into an open space, set up phone banks, and staffed them with volunteers from every part of the company—some 400 of them ultimately—24 hours a day. We gave a phone number to the media so people would know how to reach us to receive or give information about someone at the Trade Center. A group of MMC people went to major hospitals and (when it became operational) the city's family registration center to get information.

Our communications center was an unbelievable scene. While people made and took calls, messages to lost colleagues began to accumulate on the walls. We heard harrowing stories. One of our employees, a young man, had been on the elevator heading to his office on the 93rd floor. He got off at 90 and made it down. Incredibly, employees who had just been evacuated from Tower Two appeared at headquarters, asking how they could help. There were many tearful reunions.

For my part, when I could get a working phone, I contacted each of our board members to let them know what was going on. We'd had a board meeting scheduled for the following week in Germany, and we decided to move it to New York. Like millions of other people that day, I was concerned about my family's safety. With transportation down in New York, my wife had set out on foot to retrieve our children from school. They called me, in tears, when they got home. I tried to be reassuring, but it was difficult. I was in a skyscraper, looking out over dozens of trophy buildings bearing the names of America's largest companies. The TV in my office was reporting evacuations nearby; there were scores of bomb threats in midtown Manhattan during those first days. I certainly paid attention to where the fire exits were, as did everyone around me. None of us knew what might happen next.

By the end of the day on September 11, we still knew frustratingly little about the safety of our people. We had determined that 1,779 people in our various businesses had had offices in the twin towers, and another 129 were visiting there. But we were far from knowing how many had perished. It looked like it could be as many as 700.

Caring for Our People

Because of the scale of our loss and its unprecedented nature, we knew that we would need outside help. Families of missing colleagues, survivors of the attacks, and other employees would certainly have pressing emotional and other needs. We knew that we had a massive task ahead of us. We arranged for grief counselors to be available at MMC headquarters and elsewhere through the company's employee assistance program. On Wednesday, September 12, we were in touch with clinical trauma specialists and disaster counseling services that are used mostly by airlines after accidents.

By Wednesday afternoon, we knew that 1,300 of our colleagues were safe. By Friday, the number had crept over 1,400. Every confirmed survivor at that point became cause for celebration—but at the same time, the reality was dawning that no one who had arrived at work that day in Tower One had made it out. Pictures of the missing began to cover the walls. The 35th floor quickly became a living memorial—an ongoing, mass wake. It was hard to be there and harder not to be.

On Friday, September 14, we established a family assistance center at a nearby hotel to provide information, emotional support, and benefits counseling for families of missing colleagues. While the outsiders we hired helped guide our efforts, we felt strongly that our own people should staff the center, provide briefings, and meet with families.

During the week of the attacks, I saw the real strength of our community and culture and observed remarkable qualities in my colleagues. One young woman, for example, in the midst of chaos, took an active part in organizing the call center. She had been with the company for only two weeks, but she saw what needed to be done and kept her composure—that's just who she is. Fourteen people from the human resources department of Putnam, our Boston-based investment management business, jumped into a van and drove to New York to help out. It was an extraordinary act at a time when simply getting into the city was hard, and many were afraid to be here. Retirees, directors, and many other members of the MMC community volunteered to help in any way they could.

We quickly established a schedule of twice-a-day meetings to hear what was going on and make decisions. We did not restrict attendance to the meetings; people throughout the company knew that if they had information to share or needed a decision, they should be there. The meetings generally didn't last more than 40 minutes. The range of experience in the room and the openness of the exchanges helped our decision making, which was biased toward action and communication.

I made daily announcements on the emergency PA system for employees at our headquarters. To keep our colleagues around the world informed—MMC employs 58,000 people and operates in 100 countries—those announcements were posted on our Web site. (With the MMC and Marsh intranet servers destroyed in the attacks, the corporate Web site was a medium for communication with both internal and external audiences.) The announcements were also accessible by phone. On Friday, September 14, we gathered the company's 50 top executives, in person and by phone, to brief them, take questions, and hear suggestions. In our communications that first week, I referred to our progress in addressing our clients' needs and our financial situation and recovering operations, but overwhelmingly the updates were focused on people. We knew that even in our most distant locations, the foremost concern would be the same as ours in New York: What has become of our colleagues? And what are we doing to help?

After almost a week of extraordinary efforts to find people, we thought we knew the human consequences of the attacks. We also had an assessment of their impact on our business. On Sunday, September 16, I agreed to an interview with a *Wall Street Journal* reporter and said that we had lost 313 people. As it turned out, I was wrong. A number of our employees had been so shocked by their ordeal that they'd left the city or hadn't answered their phones. We were joyful when more than a dozen colleagues we had presumed lost showed up for work on Monday, September 17. We now knew that every one of our people in Tower Two had escaped. But we were left with the devastating reality that we had lost 295 members of our corporate family.

Although we had received hundreds of inquiries from the news media, the *Wall Street Journal* interview was our first (and until now our only) in-depth comment to the media. As much as we were communicating internally, our responses to press inquiries had thus far been limited. We hadn't wanted to speak publicly until we could provide a comprehensive report. Our priorities were to take care of our people and their families and to make sure our clients were well served. On Monday, September 17, the day the *WSJ* article appeared, our communications director and her team released a detailed report on our state of affairs to our principal internal and external constituencies—employees, clients, and shareholders. That same day, we published a full-page letter in major newspapers worldwide describing what we knew and what we were doing.

Running Our Business

So far, I have concentrated on our efforts to take care of people—and that was our highest priority. Those were circumstances in which people needed visible leader-ship and the comfort of community. I spent a great deal of time on the 35th floor and at the family assistance center, and I wanted to be surrounded by colleagues. At the same time, the company had other pressing needs.

We had severe challenges to address on the financial and operational fronts. In the short term, we knew we would incur heavy costs. We were in the last month of our third fiscal quarter. Our CFO directed efforts to calculate the attacks' financial consequences and how they would be reflected in the quarter's results. An early priority was to make sure that we had adequate cash and that our bank lines of credit were open. The markets were closed in the immediate aftermath of the attacks, but we soon heard they were hoping to reopen on Monday, September 17. How much disruption would they experience? Were we prepared to support our stock if necessary?

Our operations task force had its hands full—especially when we decided that we should aim not simply to repair but to improve what we'd lost in the way of systems, property, and data. All of our companies have extensive disaster recovery plans, but none had anticipated the scale, much less the precise form, of this event. We had lost the headquarters of our reinsurance subsidiary, Guy Carpenter. We had also lost some telecommunications capacity, a data center, and its servers.

In the midst of all this, we were aware of great needs on the part of our clients. Many of them had suffered losses, and virtually all of them were affected directly or indirectly by the terrorist attacks. We knew that Putnam, our investment management business, would have a bumpy road ahead when the markets reopened. Clients of Mercer, our consulting business, had new and deeper needs. But it was Marsh, our risk and insurance services business, that was facing unprecedented demand. And since Marsh had suffered the most devastating loss of people, it had the stress of dealing with client needs as its people were grieving and trying to recover. Between caring for our people and managing the business, many of us were putting in long days. We lost our sense of time. I wouldn't think about it until I looked at my watch at some point in the evening and realized I'd started my workday almost 18 hours earlier. I could see profound fatigue in the faces of my colleagues, but it didn't seem to matter to any of us because of all the things we needed to do.

Balancing Responsibilities

For me, Friday, September 28, epitomized our efforts to balance our responsibilities to people and to the business. It was the day we held our memorial service, which was attended, in person or by broadcast, by some 25,000 people. Saint Patrick's Cathedral graciously hosted the service, which included clergy representing a variety of faiths. In addition to those who could be accommodated in the nave, at least 6,000 were watching on a large screen mounted outside the cathedral. We reached employees and friends elsewhere

I wanted to make it clear that, even in mourning, we remained a proud and determined organization responsive to our clients' needs.

through closed-circuit hookups to theaters in a number of cities. It was a deeply emotional service with readings and reflections by several of my colleagues, including Jack Sinnott, the chairman of Marsh. Mayor Rudolph Giuliani also took time out of his schedule to attend and speak at the service. Expressing my feelings while maintaining my composure was as hard an assignment as I have ever had.

On the same day, MMC announced the formation of a new business. In the global marketplace of insurance sellers and large buyers, Marsh works as an adviser and broker for the buyers. The year had already been a difficult one for clients seeking affordable premiums and satisfactory terms and conditions. As we thought about our clients' needs post–September 11, it became clear that the new demand for insurance, combined with World Trade Center losses, would create conditions in which underwriters would be unable to provide enough insurance. Consequently, MMC Capital, our private equity business, sponsored and arranged financing for a new insurance provider called Axis Specialty.

It was vital for our employees, as well as our clients and shareholders, to know that we were moving ahead. I wanted to make it clear that, even in mourning, we remained a proud and determined organization responsive to our clients' needs. The juxtaposition of those events—a deeply emotional response to the human loss and a business response to the changing risk environment—reflects the balance our company has managed every day since September 11.

Because of the extraordinary talent and commitment of our people, along with the disaster recovery plans we had in place, MMC's ability to serve clients rebounded quickly after September 11, and the company has been performing well since then. But families and friends of lost colleagues cannot recover either quickly or completely from such terrible losses.

We have tried to ease the suffering of families of lost colleagues and help attend to some of their longer-term

needs. Within a week of September 11, we created the
MMC Victims Relief Fund to provide additional support
to families for their health, welfare, and education needs.
MMC contributed $20 million to the fund; employees,
clients, and others donated another $4 million. The fund
paid out virtually all the contributions to families in
February 2002.

We also established the MMC Family Relationship
Management Program, which serves as the primary
point of contact between families and the company.
Each family has been assigned a relationship manager
who helps obtain resources within and outside MMC
and who deals with individual benefits and financial,
legal, and administrative matters. The relationship managers still have regular contact with families. (See "Support for Our Families" at the end of this article.)

Four Observations

I don't know that I have enough distance from this
inconceivable event yet, or that any of us does, to give it
the historical perspective it deserves. Clearly, we have
learned some things that have affected our decisions
since. Although disaster recovery plans and dedicated
technology staff helped us restore data, critical applications, and telecommunications capabilities, we now
know it is ill-advised to locate a server farm on a high
floor of a skyscraper. We've learned not to place critical
facilities on the same power grid. We're thinking
differently about data center configuration and the sepa-
ration of IT infrastructure from applications program-
ming. Beyond such operational lessons, there are
management and other insights to be gained. I offer
these observations.

LEADERSHIP HAS ITS PLACE

In a time of crisis, there is something reassuring about
hearing the voice of a person in a position of authority,
even if the information being provided is scant. I know I
felt that way when listening to President Bush and
Mayor Giuliani in those early days. It made a difference
to people here, too, to have the company's leadership out
there communicating, constantly and informally. I don't
speak only of myself. Many of us were visible. I had help
from two past chairmen, outside directors, and retired
executives, several of whom immediately arrived to help
in whatever way they could. During one of the bomb
threats, when panic was spreading quickly through the
office, our general counsel made the difference. He didn't
have hard information to share; he simply said that he
understood people's feelings, let them know that he and I
had chosen to remain on hand, and told them we would
understand and support them if they needed to leave.
Nearly everyone stayed; his own composure had the
effect of calming others.

I cannot stress enough the importance of having a
strong group of internal and external advisers who see
things from different perspectives. We were, and still are,
dealing with problems we have never faced before, and
ideas have surfaced from all parts and levels of the company. No one person could have thought of all the things
we've done.

CULTURE COMES TO THE FORE

In a crisis, culture matters. I've related a few stories of
individual acts I admired; there were hundreds of them
that we saw or heard about later—from the MMC

employee who helped a disabled person down the stairs of Tower Two, to the many decisions made on the front lines to assist clients facing unprecedented challenges. A company's culture—ours stresses the value of people and takes pride in its reputation for service—is a crucial source of strength in a crisis.

I've also seen what a crisis can do to a culture. MMC is a multibusiness, global company—one that has made some large mergers in recent years. It's hard to create a uniform culture in such a company. But this event touched our people no matter which part of the organization or which part of the world they worked in. We all came away from it with a greater sense of belonging to the same community.

BE PREPARED TO ADAPT

It goes without saying that preparedness—good crisis management planning—is essential to being able to manage through a disaster. Our disaster recovery plans did not envision the sort of crisis we suffered or prepare us for it completely, but it very much mattered that we had those plans. We recovered all critical client data, for example, and even Guy Carpenter, whose headquarters was completely destroyed, relocated to our midtown office and other locations and was fully back in business by Monday, September 17.

But you can't anticipate the precise shape of a disaster. In a moment, the key becomes adaptability. Suddenly, our management priorities were different. We had to do things differently—for example, communicate with unaccustomed frequency and with different mechanisms. My leadership approach had to match the needs of the moment. In a crisis, you understand the need for flexibility in facing all the situations you had not anticipated.

For example, a few months after the attacks, it came to light that some victims' families were dissatisfied with the provision we had made for the continuation of health insurance. Although we considered our insurance extension to be generous, we took the criticism to heart and worked hard to understand the families' concerns. We came to see their point and amended the program.

PEOPLE'S WELL-BEING COMES FIRST

Of all the insights I can offer based on our experience, this might seem the most obvious. So many companies acknowledge their people, or at least their intellectual capital, as their greatest strength. But the crucible is a moment like September 11, when we had to make choices fast and instinctively. In the months following that day, our human resource leaders and their teams stayed close to the emerging needs of victims' families and our employees and made changes to a wide range of services and benefits. Looking back at the crisis and its aftermath, I believe that our immediate and longer-term assistance gave meaning to our commitment to people.

Past as Prologue

MMC is a company with a 130-year history, and it's a history I know fairly well. Some of the earliest stories are the most colorful—like the time our founder, Henry Marsh, boarded an ocean liner docked in New York Harbor just to get the ear of a prospective client named J.P. Morgan. He succeeded and, rather than cut short the conversation, stayed aboard while the ship embarked. Marsh had not planned for a voyage and had no luggage with him, but by the end of the trip he had U.S. Steel as a client. We recently celebrated the 100th year of that relationship and, soon after, another centennial with AT&T.

Shortly after I became chief executive, I spent some time working on a strategic review of the business. With a combination of newcomers and veterans among our executives and directors, the review needed to be grounded in a common understanding of our history and the reasons for our success over the years. MMC has grown in scale and complexity, but our long-term success is largely attributable to something very simple: a professional organization of great people. The connection between that and serving our clients with professional excellence is much of what defines us as a firm. In the darkest hour of MMC's history, I am enormously proud that our people responded to overwhelming loss by simultaneously assisting the families of lost colleagues, comforting survivors, and serving our clients.

Support for Our Families

IN THE AFTERMATH OF THE TERRORIST ATTACKS on September 11, 2001, victims' families have faced a variety of immediate needs and longer-term ones. Marsh & McLennan Companies worked quickly to provide a responsive set of benefits and services. They include:

Family Relationship Management Program. A relationship manager has been assigned to each family who lost a loved one in the attacks to serve as its single, primary point of contact. Family relationship managers help people get answers to questions and access to resources, from within MMC and through other public and private sources.

Psychological and Emotional Counseling. MMC employees and their families have access to counseling through the company's employee assistance program. The company is providing for unlimited counseling to victims' families through September 2003 and referrals to appropriate longer-term resources.

Enhanced Benefits. MMC provided a special payment equal to each lost colleague's salary for October through December 2001 and other cash benefits. Families are receiving full health insurance coverage for three years; after that, they will have access to participate in MMC's plans at their own expense for as long as they wish.

Financial Assistance. MMC contributed $20 million to establish its own Victims Relief Fund for families of lost colleagues, which ultimately attracted an additional $4 million in donations from employees, clients, and others. Contributions were dispersed to families early in 2002.

Financial Counseling. MMC has provided information to families about benefits and financial support available to them and retained an outside specialist company to provide financial counseling through March 2003. Nearly every family has met with a counselor about investment, tax, and related issues.

Family Advocacy. Among other actions, MMC petitioned the U.S. Department of Justice and members of Congress regarding proposed regulations under the September 11 Victim Compensation Fund of 2001. Each family has received an individualized 20-page dossier of work-related information about their loved one to support their application to the fund.

Remembrances. A memorial service for all MMC victims was held at Saint Patrick's Cathedral and broadcast to employees around the world. MMC hosts an electronic message board for families and friends and a virtual memorial on its corporate Web site. A permanent memorial to the victims is planned for the plaza adjacent to MMC's headquarters.

The MMC Family of Companies

MARSH & MCLENNAN COMPANIES is a global professional services firm with annual revenues of $10 billion and approximately 58,000 employees serving clients in more than 100 countries.

Marsh: Risk and insurance services

Guy Carpenter: Reinsurance services

MMC Capital: Private equity firm

Putnam Investments: Individual and institutional investment management

Mercer Human Resource Consulting: Employee benefits, compensation, communication, and actuarial services

Mercer Management Consulting: Corporate strategy and business design

Mercer Delta Consulting: Organizational transformation

National Economic Research Associates: Economic and financial analysis

Lippincott & Margulies: Brand and identity consulting

Originally published in October 2002
Reprint R0210D

The Enemies of Trust

ROBERT GALFORD AND

ANNE SEIBOLD DRAPEAU

Executive Summary

RESEARCHERS HAVE ESTABLISHED that trust is critical to organizational effectiveness. Being trustworthy yourself, however, does not guarantee that you are capable of building trust in an organization. That takes old-fashioned managerial virtues like consistency, clear communication, and a willingness to tackle awkward questions. It also requires a good defense: You must protect trust from its enemies.

Any act of bad management erodes trust, so the list of potential enemies is endless. Among the most common enemies of trust, though, are inconsistent messages from top management, inconsistent standards, a willingness to tolerate incompetence or bad behavior, dishonest feedback, a failure to trust others to do good work, a tendency to ignore painful or politically charged situations, consistent corporate underperformance, and rumors.

Fending off these enemies must be at the top of every chief executive's agenda. But even with constant vigilance, an organization and its leaders will sometimes lose people's trust. During a crisis, managers should enlist the help of an objective third party—chances are you won't be thinking clearly—and be available physically and emotionally. If you "go dark" in the face of a crisis, employees will worry about the company's survival, about their own capacity to cope, and about your abilities as a leader.

And if trust has broken down so badly that your only choice is to start over, you can do so by figuring out exactly how the breach of trust happened, ascertaining the depth and breadth of the loss, owning up to the loss instead of downplaying it, and identifying as precisely as possible the specific changes you must make to rebuild trust.

T RY AN EXPERIMENT SOMETIME. Ask a group of managers in your company whether they and their closest managerial colleagues are trustworthy and, if so, how they know. Most will claim that they themselves are trustworthy and that most of their colleagues are as well. Their answers to the second half of the question will likely reflect their beliefs about personal integrity; you'll hear things like "I'm straight with my people" or "She keeps her promises." A little later, ask them whether they think they and their colleagues are

Trust within an organization is far more complicated and fragile than trust between a consultant and a client.

capable of building trust within the organization. Because we've asked this question many times, we're pretty sure we know what you'll hear: A sizable percentage will say they have little or no confidence in the group's capacity to build and maintain trust.

What accounts for the gap between the two sets of answers? With their differing responses, the managers are simply acknowledging a fact of organizational life: It takes more than personal integrity to build a trusting, trustworthy organization. It takes skills, smart supporting processes, and unwavering attention on the part of top managers. Trust within an organization is far more complicated and fragile than trust between, say, a consultant and a client. With a client, you can largely control the flow of communication. In an organization, people are bombarded with multiple, often contradictory messages every day. With a client, you can agree on desired outcomes up front. In an organization, different groups have different and often conflicting goals. With a client, you know if there's a problem. In an organization, there's a good chance you don't, even if you're in charge. If things aren't working out with a client, either party can walk away. That's not usually an option for people in an organization, so they stick around. But if they think the organization acted in bad faith, they'll rarely forgive—and they'll never forget.

If people think the organization acted in bad faith, they'll rarely forgive—and they'll never forget.

Trust within an organization is further complicated by the fact that people use the word "trust" to refer to three different kinds. The first is *strategic trust*—the trust employees have in the people running the show to make the right strategic decisions. Do top managers have the vision and competence to set the right course, allocate resources intelligently, fulfill the mission, and help the company succeed? The second is *personal trust*—the trust employees have in their own managers. Do the managers treat employees fairly? Do they consider employees' needs when making decisions about the business and put the company's needs ahead of their own desires? The third is *organizational trust*—the trust people have not in any individual but in the company itself. Are processes well designed, consistent, and fair? Does the company make good on its promises? Clearly these three types of trust are distinct, but they're linked in important ways. Every time an individual manager violates the personal trust of her direct reports, for example, their organizational trust will be shaken.

As difficult as it is to build and maintain trust within organizations, it's critical. An established body of research demonstrates the links between trust and corporate performance. If people trust each other and their leaders, they'll be able to work through disagreements. They'll take smarter risks. They'll work harder, stay with the company longer, contribute better ideas, and dig deeper than anyone has a right to ask. If they don't trust the organization and its leaders, though, they'll disengage from their work and focus instead on rumors, politics, and updating their résumés. We know this because we've seen it happen many times and because a high percentage of consulting engagements that seem to be about strategic direction or productivity turn out to be about trust, or the lack thereof.

The building blocks of trust are unsurprising: They're old-fashioned managerial virtues like consistency, clear communication, and a willingness to tackle awkward questions. In our experience, building a trustworthy (and trusting) organization requires close attention to those virtues. But it also requires a defensive game: You need to protect trustworthiness from its enemies, both big and small, because trust takes years to build but can suffer serious damage in just a moment. We'll take a look at some of those enemies, discuss trust in times of crisis, and explore the ways to rebuild trust when it's been breached.

The Enemies List

What do the enemies of trust look like? Sometimes the enemy is a person: a first-line supervisor who habitually expresses contempt for top management. Sometimes it's knit into the fabric of the organization: a culture that punishes dissent or buries conflict. Some enemies are overt: You promise that this will be the last layoff, and then it isn't. And some are covert: A conversation you thought was private is repeated and then grossly distorted by the rumor mill. Because any act of bad management erodes trust, the list of enemies could be endless. Practically speaking, though, most breakdowns in trust that we've witnessed can be traced back to one of the following problems.

INCONSISTENT MESSAGES

One of the fastest-moving destroyers of trust, inconsistent messages can occur anywhere in an organization, from senior managers on down. They can also occur externally, in the way an organization communicates with its customers or other stakeholders. Either way, the repercussions are significant.

Consider the manager who tells employees in May that he's going to hold weekly brown-bag lunch meetings to discuss relevant issues in the marketplace. He implies that enthusiastic participation will be reflected in employees' performance reviews. But he then cancels the lunch the second, fourth, and fifth weeks because of his travel schedule. In week seven, he drops the idea entirely because, as he says, "With the summer here, we really can't count on a good turnout." When he reintroduces the idea in October and insists it will work this time, do you think his employees believe him? And when it's time for performance reviews, do you think they are confident and trusting? No. They are confused and skeptical.

Senior executives often communicate inconsistent messages and priorities to various parts of the organization. We recently worked with a major financial institution in which top executives had repeatedly told members of the marketing staff that they were full business partners of the line organizations. Most of the executives in the line organizations, however, never heard that message and continued to treat marketing employees like low-level vendors. Why didn't top management communicate a consistent message? The answer is probably some combination of what we've seen in other companies: Senior managers tell people what they want to hear. And, all too often, senior managers across business units have widely disparate worldviews, which they communicate to their constituencies.

The antidotes to inconsistent messaging are straightforward (though they are not easy to implement): Think through your priorities. Before you broadcast them, articulate them to yourself or a trusted adviser to ensure that they're coherent and that you're being honest with people instead of making unrealistic commitments. Make sure your managerial team communicates a consistent message. Reserve big-bang announcements for truly major initiatives.

INCONSISTENT STANDARDS

If employees believe that an individual manager or the company plays favorites, their trust will be eroded. Employees keep score—relentlessly. Suppose that a company's offices in one city are palatial, and in another city employees make do with cramped cubicles. Local real estate prices most likely drive local decisions, but the people who end up with the warrens feel slighted nonetheless. Or suppose that the CEO took the new vice president of marketing out to lunch when he was promoted two months ago but failed to do the same when a new head of IT was appointed last week. There might be legitimate reasons for the CEO's inconsistent behavior, but the IT executive and the people around her will jump to the least-flattering, least-legitimate conclusion. Finally, suppose that the company's star performer is allowed to bend the rules while everyone else is expected to toe the line. As an executive, you may think it's worthwhile to let the most talented employee live by different rules in order to keep him. The problem is that your calculation doesn't take into account the cynicism you engender in the rest of the organization.

MISPLACED BENEVOLENCE

Managers know they have to do something about the employee who regularly steals, cheats, or humiliates coworkers. But most problematic behavior is subtler than that, and most managers have a hard time addressing it.

Consider incompetence. Anyone who has spent time in business has encountered at least one person who is, simply and sadly, so out of his league that everyone is stupefied that he's in the position at all. His colleagues wonder why his supervisors don't do something. His direct reports learn to work around him, but it's a daily struggle. Because the person in question isn't harming anyone or anything on purpose, his supervisor is reluctant to punish him. But incompetence destroys value, and it destroys all three kinds of trust.

Then there are the people with a cloud of negativity around them. These are often people who have been passed over for promotion or who feel they've been shortchanged on bonuses or salaries. They don't do anything outright to sabotage the organization, but they see the downside of everything. Their behavior often escapes management's attention, but their coworkers notice. After a while, people tire of their negative colleagues and may even catch the negativity bug themselves.

And, finally, people who are volatile—or just plain mean—often get away with appalling behavior because of their technical competence. Extremely ambitious people, similarly, tend to steamroll their colleagues, destroy teamwork, and put their own agendas ahead of the organization's interests. In both cases, ask yourself, "Is this person so valuable to the company that we should tolerate his behavior?"

Sometimes problematic employees can be transferred to more suitable jobs; sometimes they can be coached, trained, or surrounded by people who will help them improve; and sometimes they must be let go. The point is that they can't be ignored. Every time you let troubling behavior slide, everyone else feels the effects—and blames you.

FALSE FEEDBACK

When an incompetent or otherwise unsuitable person is let go, managers often face wrongful-termination suits. "Look at these performance reviews," the supposed victim says. "They're great." And she is right: The performance reviews are great. The problem is that they're lies.

Being honest about employees' shortcomings is difficult, particularly when you have to talk to them about their performance regularly and face-to-face. But you must do it. If you don't honor your company's systems, you won't be able to terminate employees whose work is unacceptable. What's more, employees who are worthy of honest praise will become demoralized. "Why should I work this hard?" they will ask themselves. "So-and-so doesn't and everyone knows it, but I happen to know we got the same bonus." You won't hear the complaint directly, but you'll see it in the lower quality of the competent employees' work.

FAILURE TO TRUST OTHERS

Trusting others can be difficult, especially for a perfectionist or a workaholic. One top manager we worked with swore that he was going to delegate several important responsibilities. He brought in a new person at a senior level, but he was simply unable to trust her to do the work. After a few weeks, he began managing around her, issuing directives about things he had supposedly delegated and generally making her life miserable. Eventually, the manager's hoarding behavior left him isolated and hobbled. Just as important, the new employee didn't get a chance to develop professionally. Part of the implicit promise managers make is that employees will have a chance to grow. When managers don't give them that chance, the organization loses the trust of those employees, and the more talented among them leave.

ELEPHANTS IN THE PARLOR

Some situations are so painful or politically charged that it's easier to pretend they don't exist. We're talking about when someone has been fired abruptly and no one mentions it the next day at the regular staff meeting. We're talking about when an outrageous rumor finds its way to the CEO's office yet no one ever discusses it openly, even in private senior-management meetings.

Don't ignore things that you know everyone is whispering about behind closed doors. Bring such issues out into the open, explain them briefly, and answer questions as best you can. Don't be afraid to say, "I'm sorry, I can't offer more detail because that would violate a confidence." People will, sometimes grudgingly, accept the fact that they're not privy to all the gory details. But their trust in you will decline if they suspect you're trying to conceal something.

RUMORS IN A VACUUM

When a company is in the throes of a complex initiative—a new product launch, say, or the analysis of a product line that has been underperforming—there are ample opportunities for trust to break down. Employees know that something important is going on, but if they don't know the full story (maybe the full story doesn't exist yet), they'll quite naturally overinterpret any shard of information they get their hands on. Rumors circulate, and, in most cases, they'll be negative rather than positive. Temporary information vacuums in corporate life are common, and distrust thrives in a vacuum.

What can you do? Be as up-front as possible—even if that means telling employees you can't say for certain what's going to happen. And be aware that the less you say, the more likely you are to be misinterpreted.

Michael Rice, head of Prudential Securities' Private Client Group, told us of a meeting during which a group of managers proposed some structural shifts that would affect the business's operations. In response to the presentation, Rice said, "The way you've described this, you're scaring me." The room fell silent, and the meeting ended awkwardly. One of his lieutenants explained that shortly after the last time Rice had said he was scared, there had been a large layoff. People picked up on the phrase and, since Rice hadn't described his objections more fully, they overinterpreted the comment.

You don't have to be a chatterbox to counter this enemy of trust, but do try to put yourself in your listeners' shoes. What don't they know about the situation at hand, and how will that affect what they hear? Are you saying enough? Or are you speaking in shorthand, either because you feel you can't share more information or because you assume people will understand what you're getting at?

CONSISTENT CORPORATE UNDERPERFORMANCE

If a company regularly fails to meet the expectations set by its senior management team (and adopted by Wall Street), trust erodes rapidly. Look at Kodak, Polaroid, and Xerox in times of decline. When an organization's performance is weaker than expected, a growing number of employees at all levels fear for themselves on a daily basis. They spend less and less time thinking for the organization and more and more time planning their own next moves. What can you do? Be realistic when setting expectations and communicate as much as possible to all employees about why you're setting these goals and how the company can meet them. The more knowledge people have about what lies behind expectations, the more likely they are to continue trusting you and the company, even in tough times.

Trust in Tumultuous Times

As vigilant as you may be about fighting the enemies of trust that pop up in the course of doing business, there will be times when trust inside the organization is stressed to the maximum. (See "Curmudgeon's Corner" at the end of this article for more information about trust and organizational life.)

Perhaps the organization is undergoing a structural change like a merger, reorganization, or layoff (or all three). Under such circumstances, people's antennae are tuned to signals that might provide even a partial answer to the question, What does this mean for me? Memos and e-mails from senior managers, snatches of remembered conversations, phrases overheard in the parking lot—all of these are reread, rehashed, and analyzed word by word.

Don't be surprised when the things you say—including the most innocuous statements—are assigned deep, sinister meaning. People are also going to hold you accountable for what they *think* you said (which may not be what you think you said) for longer than you might believe. Consider all the organizations that announced they were "not currently planning any layoffs" but ultimately needed to reduce the workforce.

Don't be surprised when the things you say—including the most innocuous statements—are assigned deep, sinister meaning.

When the layoff is announced, employees suspect that it was in the works when the first statement was issued, and they remind senior managers about the "promise." From the senior managers' point of view, no promise was made. Technically, that's true, but that truth isn't worth much. If you want to reassure people, don't speculate about the future. Instead, treat employees like grown-ups. In the case of a layoff, share the performance data or competitive situation that makes reductions necessary. And be extremely cautious about making unequivocal statements such as the following:

- I have no hidden agenda.
- There won't be any more layoffs.
- This time we've got it fixed.
- We will be stronger as a result.
- I have total faith in the senior management team.
- This is the hardest thing I've ever had to do.

Pronouncements like these can come back to haunt you. And they probably will.

Organizations also risk losing the trust of their people in times of crisis. Whether it is an episode of violence, an accident, or a serious product flaw, a corporate crisis can have a profound effect on a company's health. Often the damage occurs not because of the incident itself but because of how it's handled internally. Company leaders, or crisis team members, become so distracted by external pressures that they don't address the crisis internally with care and attention. That's dangerous, because employees feel unsafe during a crisis. They look for reasons to trust their leaders, but they are quick to find reasons why they *can't* trust them.

Mark Braverman, a senior vice president with Marsh Crisis Consulting in Washington, DC, says companies that respond well to customers during crises very often neglect their own employees. Recovering revenues is important, as is moving the company out of the media spotlight. But calls from reporters, shareholders, and customers shouldn't be given so much attention that you ignore what's going on with the people who show up every day to work. You want things to go back to normal, so your tendency is to deal first with the people you don't "normally" have to deal with. But your people will not be able to wait until the flurry subsides. By the time you turn to them, the damage may be beyond repair.

Under extreme stress, normally competent managers may feel fragile, guilty, overwhelmed, and unable to cope. It's hard to act like a leader when you're experiencing those emotions. But employees feel just as much stress as you do, and they need calm, visible leadership far more than they normally do. If you "go dark" in the face of a crisis, employees worry about how the company will survive, about whether you're up to the task, and about their own capacity to cope. When everyone worries, trust evaporates. The first lesson here is to get yourself some help. If you were not directly affected by the crisis, you may need only a quick check-in with an objective third party. But if you were directly affected, don't assume that you are thinking clearly. Your perspective may be off. Acknowledging that fact could save you from some painful mistakes and could save employees and other stakeholders a lot of pain as well.

The second lesson is not to withdraw. Let it be known that you're aware of the situation and that you'll keep everyone posted as events unfold and as decisions are made. Set an update schedule and keep to it, even if the update is that there will be no news until next week. Just as important, be physically and emotionally accessible to the people around you. They want to know that it is okay to have feelings at work about whatever is going on. They'll look to you to set the example. And that means you have to allow yourself to do some of the things that you may have thought being a leader meant you *couldn't* do. If you're shaken, for example, say so, even as you strive to provide stable ground from which to move the organization forward. If you feel like stopping work for a few hours, or even a day, just to talk about what happened in an informal way, do it. Let people know that you are taking the time to think through what has happened, and that it is fine for them to follow suit.

Starting Over

There are times when, inevitably, trust will be badly damaged somewhere in your organization, and there's nothing you can do to stop the breakdown. Your only choice, other than finding a different job, is to rebuild. We recommend that you follow these four steps.

First, figure out what happened. That may sound simple, but it rarely is. To build your own understanding, consider these questions.

- How quickly or slowly did trust break down? If it happened fast, don't expect rapid remediation. Most of us aren't as good at forgiving as we'd like to be. If trust was lost over a period of time, it's helpful to think about the deterioration process in order to identify how to prevent such failures in the future.

- When did the violation of trust become known to you and to the larger organization? If you've known that something was amiss but failed to acknowledge the loss of trust or respond appropriately for a considerable period of time, that lag will compound employees' feelings of betrayal.

- Was there a single cause? It's easier to address a one-time event than a pattern of events, but don't be too quick to assume the problem is simple. Remember: Every organization has a few conspiracy theorists, and the perception of a conspiracy can damage trust as devastatingly as a real one can.

- Was the loss of trust reciprocal? If your trust was violated and others say that theirs was, too, chances are no one will behave fairly or objectively. It's acceptable to be angry when your trust has been betrayed. But retaliatory or vindictive? Never. We've seen organizations spiral downward as people try to hurt others who have violated their trust. If you discern that the loss of trust in your organization is reciprocal and deep-seated, a formal process of conflict resolution might be in order.

Second, when you have a reasonably good handle on what happened, ascertain the depth and breadth of the loss of trust. A sense of how much of the organization has been affected will help you avoid situations in which you try to put out a lit match with a full muster of firefighters or, by contrast, an inferno with spit. Imagine the challenges facing the management committee of Lehman Brothers after a stockbroker in a Midwestern branch was discovered to have defrauded clients out of many millions. The impact on the branch's other clients was severe, and the impact on clients elsewhere in the Midwest was also substantial. However, the reaction on the West Coast was highly varied: Many clients weren't even aware of the breach. A different level of response was required for different groups of clients.

Third, own up to the loss quickly instead of ignoring or downplaying it. Employees will be skeptical or suspicious, or both, so you'll need to choose your words carefully. But acknowledging that trust has been damaged and starting the recovery process as quickly as possible can only be to your benefit. You don't have to have all the answers or a detailed plan. There can even be a lag between naming the problem and describing what you'll do. Just let people know that you're aware of the issue and its impact on them and that you're committed to setting things right. Let them know when they will hear more from you, and stick to that time frame, even if all you can say at that point is that you're not yet ready to say anything.

Fourth, identify as precisely as possible what you must accomplish in order to rebuild trust. For example, you might need to change the relationship between people in the sales offices and people at headquarters from an adversarial one to a cooperative one. Or you might want to have people stop doing end runs around a department that has a reputation for arrogance. Then give yourself examples of what success will look like in practice. For example, "The quarterly review meetings will spend 50% less time on mediating disputes and 50% more time on planning new initiatives." Or "We will establish clear roles and responsibilities, an exceptions policy, a dispute resolution process, and submission and response protocols."

Then list the changes you'll make in organizational structure, systems, people, and culture to achieve those outcomes. What specific shifts (if any) will you make in how decisions are made, how information flows, and how it is measured, reported, compensated for, and rewarded? Should some reporting relationships be changed? Which areas might be merged, consolidated, or separated? We have seen internal rivalries dissolve almost instantaneously when competing areas come under the control of a single person. And we've been amazed at how quickly trust (and productivity) improves when the move is finally made to replace a key player who has done a poor job of building trust inside a group.

Keep an eye on practical issues: How will these valuable changes and initiatives happen? How much of the work will you do yourself, what will you delegate, and how much will be done in teams? What's a reasonable time frame for getting things done? (Some efforts will probably be ongoing, while others will be more finite.) And keep an eye on the trust recovery mission in its entirety. Very often, such missions suffer from an imbalance of short-term measures at the expense of longer-term efforts. They are also frequently tilted too much in favor of those directly affected at the expense of the broader organization. Looking hard at the plan (and asking one or two people who were not a part of its creation to scrutinize it as well) can save a great deal of time and resources down the road.

Trust within organizations isn't easy to pin down. It's hard to measure, even in a quick-and-dirty way. And suppose you could measure it perfectly—the truth is that no company would ever get a perfect score. Organizations and people are too complicated for that. Nor is it easy to define the trustworthy leader. Some exude emotional intelligence; others appear to be rather boring, extremely consistent bureaucrats. And, being human, even the best of them occasionally make mistakes that erode trust. But trust is the crucial ingredient of organizational effectiveness. Building it, maintaining it, and restoring it when it is damaged must be at the top of every chief executive's agenda.

Curmudgeon's Corner

IN WHICH WE NOTE several uncomfortable truths about organizational life

There's no such thing as a private conversation. We don't say this to make you paranoid, and maybe you have a confidant who's truly discreet. But in general you should assume that everything you say will circulate to the people who would be most affected by it.

There's no such thing as a casual conversation. People will attempt to read deep meaning into your most innocuous comments and movements.

People sometimes hear what they most fear. In some organizations, under some circumstances, people will immediately jump to the most paranoid, negative interpretation of *all* your comments and movements.

Trauma has a long half-life. You will likely find yourself apologizing for misdeeds that you did not commit and for events that occurred before you arrived.

No good deed goes unpunished. Even if you act with the purest intentions and execute with the greatest skill, someone will object to your actions or to the results you achieve.

Newton's third law doesn't always apply. Newton said that every action has an equal and opposite reaction, but you may take a small, seemingly harmless step that has a huge, negative impact. Or you may make what you think is a dramatic, deeply meaningful change, only to hear people say, "Okay, good. Now, what's for lunch?"

Originally published in February 2003
Reprint R0302G

About the Contributors

At the time this article was originally published, WARREN G. BENNIS was a Distinguished Professor of Business Administration and the Founding Chairman of the Leadership Institute at the University of Southern California in Los Angeles. He is also the author of more than twenty-five books on leadership.

DIANE L. COUTU is a senior editor at *Harvard Business Review* who specializes in articles on psychology and business. Before coming to HBR, she worked as a communications specialist for McKinsey & Company, the global management consultancy, and as a foreign correspondent for *Time Magazine* and the *Wall Street Journal Europe*. She studied literature at Yale and economics at Oxford, where she was a Rhodes Scholar. Most recently, she was an Affiliate Scholar and a Silberger Fellow at The Boston Psychoanalytic Society and Institute, Inc.

At the time this article was originally published, ANNE SEIBOLD DRAPEAU was the chief people officer at Digitas in Boston.

JANE E. DUTTON is the William Russell Kelly Professor of Business Administration at the University of Michigan. She studies how work contexts enable human thriving. Her work on compassion, resilience, and vitality at work fits the theme of positive organizational scholarship.

PETER J. FROST is the Edgar F. Kaiser Professor of Organizational Behavior at the University of British Columbia's Faculty of Commerce and Business Administration in Vancouver. His latest book is *Toxic Emotions at Work* (HBS Press, 2003).

At the time this article was originally published, ROBERT GALFORD was a managing partner of the Center for Executive Development in Boston and had taught in executive education programs at Harvard, Columbia, and Northwestern.

JEFFREY W. GREENBERG is the Chairman of Marsh & McLennan Companies, Inc. (MMC), a global professional services firm headquartered in New York. MMC is the parent company of Marsh Inc., the world's leading risk and insurance services firm; Putnam Investments, one of the largest investment management companies in the United States; and Mercer Inc., a major global provider of consulting services.

RONALD A. HEIFETZ is Cofounder of the Center for Public Leadership at Harvard University's John F. Kennedy School of Government and a principal of Cambridge Leadership Associates. His research at Harvard focuses on how to build adaptive capacity in societies, businesses, and nonprofits. His widely acclaimed book, *Leadership Without Easy Answers* (The Belknap Press of Harvard University Press, 1994), has been translated into many languages and is currently in its twelfth printing. His new book, *Leadership on the Line: Staying Alive through the Dangers of Leading*, written with Marty Linsky, was published in May 2002 by Harvard Business School Press. A graduate of Columbia University, Harvard Medical School, and the John F. Kennedy School of Government, Heifetz is both a physician and a cellist, having studied with the Russian virtuoso, Gregor Piatigorsky. Heifetz lives in the Boston area with his wife, Sousan Abadian, and their two children.

JASON M. KANOV is a doctoral candidate in the University of Michigan's Department of Organizational Psychology.

JACOBA M. LILIUS is a doctoral candidate in the University of Michigan's Department of Organizational Psychology.

MARTY LINSKY has been on the faculty of the John F. Kennedy School of Government since 1982, except for 1992–1995 when he served as Chief Secretary and Counselor to Massachusetts Governor William Weld. He is Cofounder, with Dr. Ronald Heifetz, of Cambridge Leadership Associates, a leadership consulting, training, and coaching firm. He is a consultant, facilitator, and trainer in leadership, ethics, external relations, communications, and strategic planning for a wide range of public and private sector clients in the U.S. and abroad. Linsky is a graduate of Williams College and Harvard Law School. He has been a journalist, a lawyer, and a politician, having served as a Member and Assistant Minority Leader of the Massachusetts House of Representatives. His most recent book is a coauthorship with Dr. Ronald Heifetz entitled *Leadership on the Line: Staying Alive Through the Dangers of Leading* (HBS Press, 2002). He lives in New York City with his wife, Lynn Staley, Assistant Managing Editor (Design) of *Newsweek* magazine. He has three children: Alison, Sam, and Max.

LIEUTENANT GENERAL WILLIAM G. PAGONIS is the author (with Jeffrey L. Cruikshank) of *Moving Mountains: Lessons in Leadership and Logistics from the Gulf War.*

At the time this article was originally published, SANDRA ROBINSON was an associate professor of organizational behavior at the University of British Columbia's School of Commerce and Business Administration in Vancouver, Canada.

ROBERT J. THOMAS is an associate partner and senior fellow with the Accenture Institute for Strategic Change. He is the author of *What Machines Can't Do* (University of California Press, 1994), coauthor of *Geeks and Geezers* with Warren Bennis, and is currently working on a new book for Harvard Business School Press describing how organizations can use crucibles to grow leaders.

At the time this article was originally published, MONICA C. WORLINE was a doctoral candidate in the University of Michigan's Department of Organizational Psychology.

Index